Architecting Digital Transformation

12-step Architectural Leadership Method

Dr Mehmet Yildiz

Distinguished Enterprise Architect

First Edition, September 2019
Copyright © Dr Mehmet Yildiz
Publisher: S.T.E.P.S. Publishing Australia
P.O Box 2097, Roxburgh Park, Victoria, 3064 Australia
info@stepsconsulting.com.au
Edited by Mark Longfield

Disclaimer

Table of Contents

A Modern Enterprise Architecture Approach Empowered with Cloud, Mobility, IoT & Big Data

Digital Intelligence: A framework to digital transformation capabilities

Chapter 1: Introduction

Purpose of this book

Enterprises are facing enormous challenges to respond to the rapid changes and growing demands of digital consumers globally. There is constant search to find solutions to the growing problems. The most optimal solution to address this problem is to architect our enterprise digital transformation requirements aligning with digital trends and innovative frameworks as described in this book with an articulated 12-step method.

Architecting digital transformations addresses the root causes of fundamental issues that we experience in the digital world. The proliferation of digital media in the form of images, sound, and videos created a massive demand for our infrastructure to scale globally. Relentless sharing of these media types creates an unsustainable load over the networks, applications, and other expensive infrastructure components unless an effective capacity plan is in place.

Based on my architectural thought leadership on various enterprise architecture initiatives, digital transformation, and modernisation engagements, with my accumulated body of knowledge and skills from practical settings, I want to share these learnings in a concise book with a specific 12-step method hoping to add value by contributing to the broader digital community and the progressing digital transformation initiatives.

I made every effort to make this book concise, uncluttered, and easy-to-read by removing technical jargons to make it readable by a broader audience who want to architect their digital transformation programs to align with the growing demands of their digital consumers.

In this book, I highlight the problems from an architectural point of view, following established and emerging methods, and recommend effective solutions to address them in a methodical way.

What distinguishes this book from other books on the market is that I provide a practical framework and a methodical approach to architect your organisation's digital infrastructure, applications, data, security, and other components based on experience, aiming not to sell or endorse any products or services to you.

Audience

The primary audience for this book is digital Transformation Architects who may have taken the plunge for the enormous responsibility of digitally transforming large enterprise programs. I provided an overview of the method which I developed from my experience from the field.

The messages provided in this book can also be useful for Digital Leaders, Enterprise Architects, IT Architects, IT Specialists, Program Managers, Transformation Executives including CTO- Chief Technology Officer, CDO - Chief Digital Officer, CIO - Chief Information Officer, Head of Enterprise Technologies - who engaged in and are responsible for substantial enterprise modernisation and digital transformation programs, and even CMOs (Chief Marketing Officers) who market these initiatives.

As an educative resource, this book can also be useful for students studying in disciplines related to digital technologies especially in MBA (Master of Business Administration) and Master of Technology programs.

Observations from Challenged Enterprises

Many large organisations that I work for are substantially challenged with rapid change in technology and increasing demands of consumers in this digital era. Every large organisation that I worked for affected by these changes and as an immediate reaction they initiated some digital transformation and modernisation programs to some extent at the program level or the enterprise level.

These organisations need new architectural approaches to address these issues and imminent risks. The initial modernisation and transformation initiatives help to some extent however the focus needs to be on the new projects and initiatives to adapt and respond to the growing demands. We need integral, innovative, and modern solutions for the emerging workloads.

Digital technologies span across multiple dimensions and many domains. These domains are tightly interrelated; hence, a minor change in one domain can reflect in many others. Dealing with these interrelated domains and their components require substantial restructuring.

In this book, I attempt to explain these challenges in the most straightforward format methodically and provide insights based on practical architectural thinking approach to deal with them effectively. Some of the points may sound trivial or boring from a high-level perspective, however each point I raised can have critical implications and make a significant impact on the success or failure of the enterprise to respond the growing digital demands.

I want to start with a top-down approach by introducing the method and move into the fundamentals of architecture and incrementally delve into the key framework components. Let's start with the method.

The Digital Transformation Method

Based on my decades of experience, I developed a 12-step method to architect digital transformation initiatives. Here are the components of the method which we cover each step in a distinct chapter.

1. Establish Fundamentals

2. Simplify Complexity

3. Manage Cost

4. Innovate and Invent

5. Accelerate Delivery

6. Grow with Collaboration

7. Leverage Emerging Technology & Tools

8. Reconstruct & Modernise Data

9. Mobilise Building Blocks

10. Create Smart Objects

11. Create Digital Teams

12. Reuse and Repeat

These steps are involved hence I covered in a distinct chapter with multiple sections providing an overview and delving into details for some critical ones. You can read the chapters in different orders as it suits your needs however the sections in the chapters follow a logical flow hence, I recommend reading each chapter in total unless you are looking for a specific topic to study.

Chapter 2: Establish Fundamentals

Purpose

The first pillar of our digital transformation method is establishing fundamentals. In this chapter, as fundamentals, we have an overview of architectural thinking approach within the context of architecting the digital transformation engagements.

From my experience, architectural thinking approach establishes the fundamentals and can be used as a robust framework to gain digital awareness, unfold the mystery of digital transformation, and increase our capabilities by providing a structured approach to transformation.

This structured and methodical approach can serve us as a checklist to measure our understanding of the architectural building blocks for transforming environments. The structured approach is important because our brains function using structure and patterns. Enterprise systems also are built-in and operate with structured patterns.

Using architectural thinking principles as a checklist ensures that we cover essential factors and steps in the thinking process for the digital world. This structured thinking process establishing the fundamentals can be invaluable in our enterprise-wide digital pursuits. Let's start with understanding our current situation.

Knowing Where We are

Understanding and accepting our current situation is crucial. It doesn't matter how good or bad, but we need to accept the reality as at this initial stage. The current state is our baseline and starting point. Knowing where we are can help us set our vision.

The current state for a legacy enterprise can be complex and difficult to compile. Everything is related to everything, you may even be surprised that some old systems or solutions are not documented adequately or even not at all. Therefore, we may need to conduct a gap analysis and take appropriate actions to address the gaps.

Despite all, we need to start from somewhere to identify our current environment and collect as much information as possible taking all measures. This can be one of the most painful exercises in the transformation lifecycle hence we shouldn't be discouraged. It is a necessary step and pays the dividends in the long run.

Now, that you are convinced with the importance of understanding the current situation, let's look at the big picture and touch on this important topic vision in our transformation lifecycle.

The Vision of the Solutions

In architectural thinking, any new initiative starts with a vision. In other words, as a top-down approach, architectural thinking mandates setting the vision first. Vision is being able to think about the future with creative imagination and human wisdom based on desired goals.

Vision sets the scene and shows us where we want to be in the future. Even though everyone has a vision, a productive and strategic vision is a leadership capability and requires a substantial amount of intelligence, knowledge, skills, and experience. As a digital transformation leader, I assume you have a fascinating vision for your organisation's transformational journey. We further enrich our vision by using this framework.

Practising vision in digital engagements can help us think strategically. Visionary thinking can be used to improve our intelligence as it involves multiple mental attributes and processes.

Our strategic vision needs to be realistic and convincing. We need to share it with all stakeholders and obtain their acceptance and approval. This is a crucial step that we make a real difference as a digital transformation leader.

Now that we understood the importance and necessity of vision let's move the next important point, solution strategy.

The strategy of the Solutions

Once we have a compelling vision for the digital world, it is time to set the strategy clearly. We know where we are now on the digital journey and strive for where we want to go. Our destination needs to be marked. Our digital strategy helps us reach our destination using a master plan. The master plan can be a high-level roadmap to take us to the destination we set. We need to proceed with a clear strategic roadmap otherwise we can get lost in the details and the constant noise.

Similar to visionary thinking, strategic thinking also can help us enhance our digital capabilities as far as our strategies related to digital matters such as the adoption of digital progress leading to transformation. Our digital strategy can pose many requirements.

Requirements of the Solutions

Digital endeavours can pose many requirements. Requirements can be interrelated and have multiple facets. Most of the time, requirements can be seen simple, however they are not easy to deal with.

Therefore, we need to make a concerted effort to understand the requirements from all angles in a structured way. Requirements involve multiple processes and stakeholders. These stakeholders can be from different parts of the organisation with varying goals, roles and responsibilities. We need to identify them.

Both users and systems have their unique and common requirements. There are different requirements for different kinds of users — for example, internal and external users, technical, executive, and management users can pose different requirements. Systems also can have their unique requirements.

The system requirements can be categorised under technical, support, and operational requirements. In architectural terms, requirements can be classified under two main categories, namely, functional and non-functional.

The functional requirements of a solution involve what the system offers to the consumers as functionality to be accomplished. For example, the system may offer calculations, data processing, or workflows. Functional requirements are usually related to the consumers of the solution. They describe what the consumers expect from the solution product and services.

Non-functional aspects involve how the solutions can accomplish these functionalities, such as their performance, availability, security, reliability, scalability, usability, configuration, scalability and many more. These are primarily technical and operational requirements. The tasks involved in the Non-Functional requirements usually relate to the IT support and maintenance teams.

Requirements gathering for digital endeavours are an end to end process such as collecting, analysing, clarifying, tracking, validating, and using them. As practical guidance, we use the acronym SMART to characterise requirements. SMART stands for specific, measurable, actionable, realistic and traceable. These five attributes can help increase the quality of requirements. To better understand requirements, especially from the user perspective, we need to deal with use cases.

Use Cases of the Solutions

Related to requirements, understanding the use cases for digital transformation solutions are essential architectural thinking skills. Dealing with use cases require different thinking modes, such as looking at things from the user's perspective. Observing and being an observer at the same time is a critical mental capability.

More specifically, a use case is a specific situation depicting the use of a product or service of a solution by the consumers. We develop use cases from the users' perspective. We need to understand how the consumers are intended to be using a particular component or aspect of the solution.

Usually, the functional requirements can help us to formulate the use cases. Alternatively, in some circumstances, use cases help formulate the functional requirements. Use cases and requirements are interrelated. We need to analyse them together; not in isolation.

Some selected users can help us understand the use cases when we interact with them. We need to ask questions to specific users and obtain their feedback on how they are intended to use a specific function that is expected to be in the solution document as a building block in the overall solution document.

In general, overall solution use cases need to be defined and elaborated with the input from all stakeholders of the solution; not just end-users. There may be different use cases for different stakeholders of the solution.

Use cases can also be determined based on roles and personas in a solution. Personas represent fictitious characters based on our knowledge of the users in the solution. Identifying personas and use of them in our use case development and requirements analysis can be beneficial.

While dealing with use cases, requirements refinement continues as a parallel activity in the subsequent phases. We need to ensure that we follow a pragmatic approach to the requirements phase. Let's be mindful that a perfectionist approach can consume a large amount of our limited budget which is common and an undesirable situation for digital transformation initiatives.

Once we handled the requirements at a reasonable amount and integrate them with the use cases of the solution, we can move into setting the current and future state as a critical artefact of our digital transformation solution.

Current and Future State of Solution

After understanding the requirements and clarifying the use cases of the solution, we need to apply them to the current state. The current state shows us where we are now as discussed in the first step.

By understanding the current state and its requirements to transform, we set future state and develop a roadmap to reach the target transformation goals. The future state requires a substantial amount of analysis and predictions. In this phase, we can consult multiple subject matter experts to ensure the future state reflects our vision, mission, and solution strategy; and ensure that it meets identified requirements.

This architectural thinking approach for understanding the current environment and setting the future state applies to any digital solution that we engage on a daily basis. This structured approach is instrumental for the success of our digital transformation initiatives. Once we set the future state, the next critical step is the assess feasibility of the solution for the construct, deployment, and consumption goals.

Architectural Feasibility

Architectural thinking can guide us to think the feasibility of our digital solution roadmap by looking at the risks, dependencies and the constraints on the way.

The feasibility is practised using a viability assessment work-product which is a template covering all aspects of our solution from operability perspective. We can either use a viability work-product template from an established method such as TOGAF or our organisation's proprietary method.

Beware that the viability assessment can be categorised under different names. To ensure, we may check which work product is used in our proprietary method to capture risks, issues, assumptions and dependencies.

Developing a comprehensive viability assessment can help us mitigate critical risks, resolve existing issues, capture assumptions, address challenging dependencies, and possible interdependencies. Missing this critical step in our digital solution approach can result in dire consequences in the long run. Therefore, this is a mandatory step in the solution lifecycle.

Most of the time, assessing viability also require making a considerable number of trade-offs to reach optimal solution outcomes. Let's understand what an architectural trade-off is.

Architectural Trade-offs

When architecting digital solutions, we make substantial amounts of trade-offs. When making trade-offs, we need to consider critical factors, such as cost, quality, functionality, usability, and several other non-functional items such as capacity, scalability, performance, usability, and security.

We make trade-offs to create a balance between two required yet incompatible items. In other words, a trade-off is a compromise between two options. For example, it is possible to make a trade-off between quality and cost for particular items.

Sometimes, dealing with trade-offs can pose a dilemma. We may tear ourselves between two competing and compelling options. In these circumstances, we must revisit our priorities. Re-examining our priorities, especially set by the key stakeholders for the solution objectives, can provide us useful clues and necessary guidance. In addition, we can also revisit our approved vision, mission, and solution strategy as sometimes our memories may fail to remember exact details in the rapid-paced transforming environments.

There may also be times that we make some of the architectural trade-offs to deal with uncertainties and ambiguities. To deal with these types of trade-offs, we can use techniques such as comparing and contrasting situations and taking calculated risks.

It is not possible to develop an architectural solution without taking risks. It is also possible that these risks can be turned into opportunities hence we need to mitigate them methodically and measurably. Now let's discuss the next critical point which is architectural decision.

Architectural Decisions

Each trade-off requires to be supported by some architectural decisions. These crucial decisions can have substantial implications for the success or failure of our digital solutions.

We need to make architectural decisions very carefully and measurably. Each decision can have a severe impact and multiple implications on the solution outcomes. It may be costly to change the architectural decisions at later phases of the solution lifecycle.

Some implications can be cost-related or compliance constraints, while others can relate to non-functional aspects such performance, scalability, capacity, availability, security or usability.

In addition, our architectural decisions must be validated with subject matter experts and communicated with multiple stakeholders for their acceptance and approval to reach the optimal consensus on the validity of the decision.

Architectural Context

After making the architectural decisions and obtaining necessary approvals, the next challenging task is to provide a representative picture of the solution in a single page. This illustrated representation is usually called the solution context showing the critical dependencies. Solution context is a work-product template which can be found in many established methods as a sample.

Creating a solution context requires abstracting skills. We need to represent a large volume of information in small pictures by setting concise relationships amongst the components. We can apply the proverbial principle of one thousand words in a single picture.

This abstract thinking skill is an example of architectural intelligence that we add to the digital transformation solution process. Setting the context for any solution can help us communicate it to relevant stakeholders in an understandable manner. Context adds clarity to understanding the overall solution.

Architectural Models

We need to develop multiple models for digital transformation solutions. Models are essential work-products in architectural solutions. A model is the proposed structure typically on a smaller scale than its original.

Once we draft a specific solution at an abstract level and our stakeholders understand it, the next important step in the architectural thinking process is to represent the abstract level in further details by describing each component and the relationships.

Describing abstract representations in concrete details also requires a great deal of mental exercise, including dealing with multiple patterns, which can stimulate our thinking abilities.

Some of the vital Architectural models which we can apply to the potential modernisation solutions are Component Model, Operational Model, Performance Model, Security Model, Availability Model, Services Model and Cost Model.

These models need to be precisely documented, reviewed by the domain architects and governed by the Architecture Board or a Design Authority in the organisation. You can find samples of these models in established methodologies searching the names provided in the previous paragraph.

Documentation of the architectural models can include both textual explanations and practical diagrams. For example, for a Component Model, all components and their relationships can be clearly illustrated in a diagram. The components and their functions can also be explained in detail. Some of the architects use their own proprietary architectural tools or PowerPoint, I personally use Visio as a tool to create my Component and Operational Models and share the output as a PDF to the relevant stakeholders.

The architectural diagrams can be useful communication tools for the selected models because the governance process for handling the solution architecture models requires presenting them to the Architecture Board or a Design Authority.

With an effective presentation and articulated communication, obtaining technical assurance approvals can be faster and easier. Otherwise, people in these forums struggle to understand the key points and consume substantial amounts of time to approve them.

Approval for some of these models may also need to be obtained from the financial, commercial and other business stakeholders. For example, the Cost Model, the Services Model, and the Availability Model can have content that requires financial or commercial approval at enterprise level.

Let's remember that we not only deal with the architectural and technical aspect of the digital transformation solutions but also the financial and commercial aspects. We also collaborate with multiple architects in transformation programs who create several models using the best architectural practices.

High-Level Designs

Once the architectural models are developed, we need to create fundamental high-level designs. Digital transformation initiatives require the development of multiple work-products covering high-level designs based on the solution context.

Use of fundamental high-level designs to see the big picture for each solution building block can be instrumental to digital transformation solutions. The high-level design needs to be well understood, accepted and approved by all stakeholders. Let's be mindful that at the later stages of the solution lifecycle, it can be very difficult and costly to change these designs.

To this end, we ensure that the high-level designs are produced using our strategy and roadmap and fully aligned for reaching the goals of the optimal solution.

Detailed Designs and Specifications

Like any other enterprise IT system, modernisation and transformation solutions are expected to deliver all their detailed designs and specifications correctly. Applying a comprehensive configuration management practice for solutions components can be effective and useful when dealing with specifications.

In digital transformation solutions, a specification can be defined as the act of precisely identifying the enterprise ecosystem items. Since specifications require precision, delivering the right specification is an essential requirement for enterprise applications and their associated critical business and emergency responses.

System specifications need to be accurate, reliable and fast when collecting data, communicating information, sharing data and making accurate decisions. Unreliable communication of the specifications by various silos, inaccurate decisions made by those specifications, their cumbersome layout can lead to disastrous results when attempting to detail the digital transformation solutions.

Finding inaccurate detailed designs or wrong specifications during the implementation and production support phase can be very cost-prohibitive due to massive re-work requirements. These unexpected errors shatter the whole solution from every angle and as digital transformation architects we are the first ones who kept responsible for the consequences.

In addition to rework, the implications for SLAs can also cause a considerable amount of financial loss to the organisation. Rework is identified as one of the most critical lessons learned from the failed digital transformation projects. Therefore, we need to ensure our detailed designs and related specifications are accurate and verified by relevant subject matter and domain experts.

As lead transformation architects, we set and chair the design authority for the digital transformation programs within our responsibility areas. We must closely work with the solution architects, domain architects, technical specialists, and solution designers. We cannot afford any silos in high-level and detail design phases. It must be a fully integrated and collaborative team under our technical and architectural leadership.

Dynamic and Flexible Governance

Technical governance is an essential aspect of digital transformation initiatives. These transformation programs require particular governance model due to their nature. A dynamic and flexible governance model is essential for transformation initiatives.

The traditional stringent and extreme rule-based or oppressive governance models can be roadblocks to the progress. From my experience, agile principles best suit the dynamic governance models. We further discuss this point in the chapter titled "Accelerate Delivery".

Governance committees in digital transformation programs can be complicated and sophisticated at multiple levels. There are many roles and responsibilities for governance committees. For example, transformation architects can run the architecture review boards or design authority forums established for complex digital transformation programs.

Domain Architects, Technical Specialists, or Subject Matter Experts verify technical accuracy in their domains and expertise areas. There may be multiple of these professionals attending the governance forums.

In addition, sponsoring executives can join these forums every now and then and look at the financial and commercial aspects of the solutions. Program managers always attend every governance forum and are responsible for the compliance and risk management of the solutions.

We can use several governance frameworks based on our solution domains. One of the common frameworks for technical governance in the industry is COBIT (Control Objectives for Information and related Technology). Use of frameworks like COBIT can help organisations gain optimal value from their IT investments by maintaining a balance between gaining benefits and optimising risk levels and resource use. There can be other governance model based on the industry which enterprise belongs and adheres.

This chapter concludes the high-level architectural fundamentals that we can use in our 12-step transformation method. In the next chapter, we delve into the next step, digital complexity which is another important topic related to digital intelligence. In the meantime, take a quick look at the following take away points to reinforce your learning from this chapter.

Chapter Summary and Take Away Points

Architectural thinking approach establishes the fundamentals and can be used as a robust framework to gain digital awareness, unfold the mystery of digital transformation, and increase our capabilities by providing a structured approach to transformation.

The structured approach is important because our brains function using structure and patterns.

Understanding and accepting our current situation is crucial.

Despite all, we need to start from somewhere to identify our current environment and collect as much information as possible taking all measures.

Vision sets the scene and shows us where we want to be in the future.

Our strategic vision needs to be realistic and convincing. We need to share it with all stakeholders and obtain their acceptance and approval.

Our digital strategy helps us reach our destination using a master plan. The master plan can be a high-level roadmap to take us to the destination we set. We need to proceed with a clear strategic roadmap otherwise we can get lost in the details and the constant noise.

Both users and systems have their unique and common requirements. The system requirements can be categorised under technical, support, and operational requirements. In architectural terms, requirements can be classified under two main categories, namely, functional and non-functional.

The functional requirements of a solution involve what the system offers to the consumers as functionality to be accomplished.

Non-functional aspects involve how the solutions can accomplish these functionalities, such as their performance, availability, security, reliability, scalability, usability, configuration, scalability and many more.

We use the acronym SMART to characterise requirements. SMART stands for specific, measurable, actionable, realistic and traceable.

A use case is a specific situation depicting the use of a product or service of a solution by the consumers. We develop use cases from the users' perspective.

Use cases can also be determined based on roles and personas in a solution. Personas represent fictitious characters based on our knowledge of the users in the solution.

By understanding the current state and its requirements to transform, we set future state and develop a roadmap to reach the target transformation goals. The future state requires a substantial amount of analysis and predictions.

The feasibility is practised using a viability assessment work-product which is a template covering all aspects of our solution from operability perspective.

Missing this critical step in our digital solution method can result in dire consequences in the long run.

We make trade-offs to create a balance between two required yet incompatible items. In other words, a trade-off is a compromise between two options.

Re-examining our priorities, especially set by the key stakeholders for the solution objectives, can provide us useful clues and necessary guidance.

It is not possible to develop an architectural solution without taking risks. It is also possible that these risks can be turned into opportunities hence we need to mitigate them methodically and measurably.

We need to make architectural decisions very carefully and measurably. Each decision can have a severe impact and multiple implications on the solution outcomes. It may be costly to change the architectural decisions at later phases of the solution lifecycle.

Creating a solution context requires abstracting skills. We need to represent a large volume of information in small pictures by setting concise relationships amongst the components.

Some of the vital Architectural models which we can apply to the potential modernisation solutions are Component Model, Operational Model, Performance Model, Security Model, Availability Model, Services Model and Cost Model.

Use of fundamental high-level designs to see the big picture for each solution building block can be instrumental to digital transformation solutions.

System specifications need to be accurate, reliable and fast when collecting data, communicating information, sharing data and making accurate decisions.

Finding inaccurate detailed designs or wrong specifications during the implementation and production support phase can be very cost-prohibitive due to massive re-work requirements. These unexpected errors shatter the whole solution from every angle and as digital transformation architects we are the first ones who kept responsible for the consequences.

The traditional stringent and extreme rule-based or oppressive governance models can be roadblocks to the progress.

One of the common frameworks for technical governance in the industry is COBIT (Control Objectives for Information and related Technology).

Chapter 3: Simplify Complexity

Purpose

The second pillar in our method is dealing with enterprise complexity. Dealing with complexity requires extensive architectural capability and substantial input to the solution.

Considering the context of digital transformation, the purpose of this chapter is to point out the complexity as one of the most significant challenges related to digital engagements. To this end, we need to find ways to architect simplicity.

Once we understand the complexity and embrace it as a reality, the next step is to find effective ways to deal with complexity. As you may guess already, from an architectural standpoint, I'd propose a structured approach to deal with complexity. Let's deep dive to overcome this critical architectural obligation!

Enterprise Environments

We know that enterprise environments can be extremely complex with multiple layers of systems, subsystems, technology stacks, tools, and processes coupled with numerous stakeholders with different agendas and consumers with different expectations.

Even though the systems, tools, processes and technology stacks can be challenging, the more significant part of the iceberg, the real challenge, is dealing with people in the enterprise, especially multiple stakeholders with different roles, responsibilities, and confusing agendas.

As a result, coupling systems and people can add extra complexity to the enterprise environments. Therefore, we must find effective ways to manage enterprise complexity for our digital transformation programs.

Managing Complexity

Fortunately, there are different approaches and techniques to manage complexity in enterprises transforming to digital goals. In this section, as a jumpstart, I provide a generic approach commonly used by transformation architects to deal with enterprise complexity.

The most common technique is simplifying complexity by using a partitioning approach. This technique applies to both systems and people. To simplify complexity, we can divide, subdivide, segregate, or apportion the systems, objects, or components, or teams to smaller units.

The process of partitioning refers to making smaller parts of an astronomical object like a transforming enterprise. Let's say that we are dealing with an extensive network system in the organisation. Dealing with such an extensive system can be daunting. In this case, we partition the overall network to smaller parts such as a wide-area network or a local-area network. Then we can further partition the wide-area network from tools and technology stacks perspectives such as routers, switches and other devices. Then, dealing with the segmented system can be more efficient and faster.

Once we partition an overarching system, then we can start simplifying it by looking at the quantity. Another way of simplifying a system is reducing the number of repetitive constituents. Take the number of servers, for example, looking at a thousand units of servers, and ten servers can make a massive difference. Reducing numbers can be useful to simplify quantitative components.

Another technique could be moving an item from a large group of the clustered items but still, keep the relationship to preserve its core identity. We cover the importance of simplification for enterprise digital transformations a critical success factor in subsequent sections of this chapter.

After partitioning and simplifying, another useful method is iterating. Probably you heard a lot about this term while working with agile methods and in agile teams. It is kind of a buzzword in agile teams. Iteration is progressing activities in smaller steps and chunks. Iteration is one of the best-proven approaches to deal with complexity and uncertainty.

Moving with iterative steps, we can achieve some small results. If the small result is positive, we make progress and go to the next iteration. If the result is negative, we fail but learn how not to do this specific action and try another iteration. It can be resembled babies to learn walking experientially.

The positive side of this negative result is that we fail cheap, and we fail quickly. Failing cheap and quickly don't make a big difference from a financial, commercial or project schedule perspectives. Paradoxically, failing cheap and quick provide financial gains. We learn quickly, deal with uncertainly efficiently, and move faster to create better results for our solutions goals.

Just a quick memory trick, we can remember these three basic methods using daily examples such as we have separate teams for different functions at work; this is partitioning of teams. We only belong to a single nation; this is a simplification. We plan for a school or certification exam chapter by chapter; this is iteration. There are also different tools that we use for these techniques. We cover them in the subsequent section of this chapter.

Purpose for Simplicity

Simplicity is a substantial requirement to be fulfilled for digital transformations and modernisation goals. Simplicity is also one of the critical attributes of digital transformation leaders. Digital transformation leaders must be capable of turning complexity to simplicity. Let's touch on the reasons briefly.

Simplicity touches almost every angle of transformation solutions, as these solutions can incredibly be complex. Simplicity, in sophisticated enterprises, is a paradoxical topic.

Enterprise modernisation and transformations are complex tasks and require sophisticated intelligence such as in-depth knowledge, varied skills, and extensive experience. We must simplify the complicated processes, systems, tools and technologies using our architectural capabilities.

Paradoxically, to create simplicity, one needs to deal with a lot of complexity, complications and sophisticated matters. This is where architectural capabilities play an important role. Obtaining the required knowledge, acquiring advanced skills, and gaining substantial experience are not easy and not indeed trivial activities. We need to deal with complexity using our digital intelligence to create simplicity.

From my observations, digitally intelligent transformation architects who deal with complexity and sophisticated matters can have extraordinary attributes to simplify things for other people. At the most fundamental level, creating simplicity requires effective communication.

Simplicity is a well sought-after characteristic in digital services and products. The modern digital world aims to offer simplified solutions to consumers. As opposed to complexity, simplicity is favourable by consumers. Therefore, digital transformation leaders are expected to simplify complex situations and complicated problems and offer simple solutions. Communication simplicity is one of the critical factors; hence, we emphasise it in the next section.

Communication Simplicity

As transformation architects and digital leaders, we are expected to articulate the most complicated and complex matters in a simple format that is understandable by all stakeholders. This is a fundamental architectural capability.

Creating simplicity for communication requires in-depth knowledge, flexible thinking, and demonstrated skills in articulation. Simplicity requires crystal clear communication. One way of clear communication is to customise our message to people's level and the right context we communicate. This requires thinking on our feet at all times.

Simplicity is a desired attribute for dealing with technical matters and building relationships. We must communicate in simple terms refraining from convoluted sentences, technical jargons, and myriad of acronyms.

When we use an acronym, we always should provide the meaning of acronym to maintain clarity. We cannot assume that everyone understands the acronym we use. Some stakeholders can be intimated by use of acronyms hence we need to be mindful of this situation.

We need to simplify technical matters when dealing with technical issues in diverse forums. One way of simplifying technical matters is use of metaphors or practical examples.

We must establish relationships that depict simplicity and efficiency with our stakeholders in our actions. This simplified communication approach can make us more credible and create a perception of trustworthiness and help us communicate our message more effectively.

User-Centric Simplicity

Simplicity requires to ask the question of how we can create products and services simple, intuitive, and human-centric. The consumer-oriented simplicity is a requirement for leading innovative teams in the digital transformation initiatives.

As mentioned in previous section, as Transformation Architects and Digital leaders, with this capability, we need to motivate our teams to think in simple user-centric terms when conveying our messages for complicated technical processes.

We understand that the path to digital transformation begins with simplifying the systems, tools, technology, and process components at all levels and layers. User centricity is the factor in achieving this goal.

One of the effective ways to simplification for user-centricity is automating routine tasks and repetitive technology stacks. Automation can help standardise and simplify convoluted and repetitive tasks prone to human errors. In the simplest terms, reducing human errors can increase user satisfaction. While delving into details in technology, we also need to focus on emerging needs by simplifying them in consumer terms.

In general, consumers keep complaining that technology creates complexity and make it difficult to understand concepts and objects in natural human language. For example, many consumers complain about the cumbersome documentation written in a convoluted language.

I witnessed that some consumers also show their disapproval for voluminous of documents for the use of a small technology device. They call it a waste as most of the time they ignore them. We need to be mindful of providing concise information in the right context and use cases.

Process Simplicity

Process simplicity is a crucial activity we undertake as transformation architects. We can start with the cultural aspects and user point of views in the enterprise. This can be a good starting point to tackle our convoluted processes.

From a cultural standpoint, I observed a generational disconnect in dealing with processes in numerous enterprises. For example, the old generation used to read manuals to solve their computer problems. Software stacks used to come with large read-me files. There were hundreds of pages of process documents that we needed go through.

However, the new generation in these enterprises works with technology intuitively. They hardly look at product or process manuals. If they are stuck, they would usually watch a YouTube video on how to do something or how to troubleshoot something. Instead of reading, they prefer watching a video. We need to be mindful of this dramatic cultural shift in consumer technologies and modernise our processes based on consumer trends.

We need to have a specific mission to simplify the business and technology processes and make them user-centric. This effort aims at efficiency and effectiveness of technology products and services leading to digital transformation goals.

Technology simplification is another critical point while addressing process modernisation. Technology is rapidly transforming towards service orientation. Most of the technology domains are provided based on services models.

The most common technology trend is the Cloud services model. In the Cloud services model, everything is provided as services. For example, cloud service models can be infrastructure, platform, and software as a service. Indeed, many other technology stacks and processes such as data analytics and business processes can be offered as simplified services.

The sophisticated services model in the back office requires substantial amounts of simplification for users to take benefits of using complicated technologies. We can add value to the business by simplifying the processes of these services for the team members in our transformation programs.

We must inspire our architectural and design team members to simplify all process documents by empathising with consumers. Simplification is an innovative process that we must lead as role models.

Simplicity and clarity are closely related. Especially in the technical services industry, providing a transparent experience to the technical team members can be very beneficial. Besides, making this transparent experience available to the end-user even more simplified and more explicit formats for the usage patterns can add additional value to the service provision goals.

An effective way of simplifying our processes and providing simplicity to the consumer is to think like the consumers. We must keep focusing on the core tenets of simplifying the process of our products and services for the best possible user experience and satisfactory consumption merits.

Design Simplicity

Design simplicity is an essential factor to consider in digital transformation goals. Design simplicity has a tremendous impact on the subsequent phases of the transformation lifecycle, such as service delivery and support. The simpler the design, the more effective the delivery and service support can be.

Applying design thinking, combined with adopting agile methods for design, is one of the simplification approaches. Simplification is an enabler for accelerated service delivery. Agile methods strive for simplifications using an iterative approach. Progressing with iterations can be simpler than progressing with whole chunks.

By applying agile methods to the design phase, complicated requirements and solution processes are simplified using simple use cases based on personas and design flaws can be addressed rapidly.

By using an agile approach, complex systems can be deconstructed to smaller parts and dealt with simpler chunks. We can simplify system relationships with iterative flows. Our simplifying focus for designs must be on smaller building blocks.

Most of the technology services nowadays are digitally offered using mobile devices such as tablets and smartphones. For example, our mobile designs must focus on simplicity by removing clutter from screens due to the nature of small screen views. These types of designs must focus on only fundamentally essential objects. These activities are fundamental considerations for digital transformation goals.

Designing complex systems also require simplifications through modular and service-oriented designs. Modularity and modular approaches to complex solutions are essential for design simplification, modernisation, and digital transformation goals.

One of the approaches for the transformation goals in design simplification can be a domain-based walkthrough of simplifying modules of IT infrastructure, applications, architecture, middleware, security, network, and data domains.

To elaborate on design simplification in the technology domain, let's take containers as an example. Containers break down monolithic interdependent architectures into manageable, and independent components. A container, as a loosely coupled system, is an entire runtime environment in a bundle. It includes dependencies, binaries, libraries, and configuration files. These new techniques and approaches help us simplify the design process.

As transformation architects, we must be conscious of simplicity for our designs and work with our designers closely. To achieve this goal, we can run workshops to convey the message for the intuitive user-centric designs based on simplicity principles. We normally don't design but we facilitate design activities demonstrating our informed leadership.

Specification Simplicity

Convoluted specifications can be troublesome and require substantial simplification for digital transformation goals. We can engage multiple specialists, subject matter experts, and domain architects to help us to simplify our specifications.

For many years, we spent time and energy on the system and user specification of software and hardware products. Creating voluminous of specifications cost an enormous amount of funds for our projects developing the specifications with many engineers, architects, and technical specialists. However, it is evident that the investment we make on these convoluted specifications yields in little gain than expected.

The digital trends, mobile culture and agile approaches made substantial changes in addressing the cumbersome specifications, especially concerning the users or consumers. The deep-down technical details for user specifications are found unnecessary. Agile methods propose simplifications of cumbersome specifications delivering in user stories format.

User stories are simple templates, including the functionalities, capabilities, and specifications from users or consumers point of view. Developing and understanding the user stories consist of a single page can be much more comfortable and more effective than developing or reading hundreds of pages of specifications in traditional methods.

Simplicity for Technical Language

Simplicity is also essential for technical communication. Effective technical communication requires substantial simplification. The simplification process for communication enables to facilitate understanding of issues, risks and dependencies effectively.

Simplified communication is a challenging task; however, we can apply it to our day-to-day interactions by using specific rules and techniques. We can translate complex problems into clear messages that can be acted on or executed with simplicity and agility.

Refraining from convoluted phrases and instead, use of precise language and explicit statements are essential factors in simplifying communication. Even though we may have an extensive vocabulary and broad range of technical terms, particularly in-depth knowledge of technical matters, we need to be able to use simple language to pass our message to non-technical people's level.

For example, we can use customised terms and references while speaking to a manager, a secretary, an executive, a salesperson, and a technician. We can customise our message as needed in a specific context.

While we can use advanced business terms to senior executives to articulate a point, we need to use deep technical terms to talk with engineers, subject matter experts, or technical specialists. This awareness, customisation, and flexibility in communication is mandatory for us to convey our critical message.

The attention span for our generation is relatively low due to many technical disruptions in our lives. To this end, we must get to the point quickly before losing the attention of people. For example, we may use lively words to illustrate a technical situation rather than using abstract terms and jargons.

Simplicity in written technical communication is essential too. People don't have much time and brainpower to understand intricate details in our technical documents. When authoring a document, we must be sharp and to the point with clear statements. As a principle, short sentences are always preferable to improve readability and hold attention span or readers.

The main benefit of simplification for oral and written technical communication is to pass the desired message effectively in the shortest possible time. It is beneficial to refrain from jargons, big words and complex sentence structures in oral and written communication.

Being able to articulate a situation in the simplest possible terms also can increase the confidence of the target person when dealing with digital transformation leaders. This capability is essential for the success of our digital transformation goals.

The right context in simplifying the technical language is also required. It is essential to balance qualitative and quantitative aspects while conveying a technical message to a broader audience. We must be context-aware and deliver our message in the right context.

It is imperative that we need to strive to articulate the business value proposition to the business stakeholders rather than showing off our technical eminence detailing convoluted details. Many transformation architects are told off when they delve into unnecessary technical details with senior transformation executives.

Governance Simplicity

Simplicity for governance also matter. Complex and complicated governance processes and procedures can be a hurdle for enterprise digital transformation initiatives. These complex governance processes can cause delays, confusions, rework, and consequently low performance for the transformation goals.

Because of these known implications, it is critical to simplify governance framework, process and procedures for these initiatives. We must be aware of the importance of governance and pay special attention to the required rigour.

We cannot compromise the quality requirements in governing technology solutions. However, while having this architectural rigour, we also need to have a balance for delivering the message in the simplest possible terms and making the processes for governance in the most effective ways.

As digital governance leaders, we must stay on top of technology trends and developments to govern them for transformation goals. As part of our governance role, we need to ensure all technology practices adhere to regulatory standards in our enterprise industries. Let's be mindful that there may be varying industry regulation requirements in different enterprises.

Data Simplicity

Data simplification is a widely discussed topic in digital transformation environments. One way of simplifying data is to clean it, remove duplications and errors. Reducing data sources and volumes, when needed, are also used to simplify and streamline data management processes.

However, there is a paradoxical situation to point out for data volumes as far as simplicity is concerned for digital transformation. For example, more data is believed to create complexity; however, this is not necessarily true. It is just the opposite situation for digitally transforming environments. Since we have more and richer data to feed the systems, the systems can produce better output with increased data sets.

We can achieve data simplicity through the right data analysis, intelligence, powerful tools, and effective management strategies. In other words, when correctly and purposefully analysed, more data can add better intelligence for modernising and transforming the data platforms.

We need to understand the importance of data for transformation initiatives and use established techniques and evolving methods in data science. We can leverage the industry knowledge and focus on simplifying data collection, process, management, storage and analytics.

Besides, for enterprise modernisation and transformation purposes, the traditional data management methods cannot suffice; therefore, we need to consider Big Data management technologies, process and tools for this simplification process.

One of the simplified Big Data trends in massive digital transformation and modernisation initiatives is the use of Cloud services for Big Data solutions. There is even a specific Big Data as a Service model that we can consider in our specific workload transformation goals. The next point in our simplification list is presentation.

Presentation Simplicity

We also need to simplify our presentations for effectiveness of our message to broader communities. We may need to provide many presentations to different stakeholders for enterprise modernisation and transformation initiatives. We present to multiple groups using PowerPoint slides or Visio images. We need to use these tools very carefully to maintain the focus of the audience and effectively convey critical messages.

Dead from PowerPoint is a famous statement depicting inefficiencies of presentations using an excessive number of slides and just reading the points from the slides. Being brief and concise in presentations is also an essential simplification method for effective communication.

For example, we can simplify team presentations by cutting unnecessary, irrelevant details and using a concise number of slides focusing on necessary points when using a PowerPoint as a tool. The core message must be kept in mind at all times.

Another crucial consideration is focusing on conveying the intended central message rather than trying to impress the audience with sophisticated communication techniques. Endless discussions may cloud the essential message; therefore, it is critical to control the presentation process and focus sharply on the essential points in our presentations.

We can provide simplified, clear and concise presentations without compromising the quality of content and effectiveness of the message. We also can encourage the team members to follow simplicity principles in our presentations and provide constant constructive feedback to maintain this simplicity culture.

Chapter Summary and Take Away Points

We know that enterprise environments can be extremely complex with multiple layers of systems, subsystems, technology stacks, tools, and processes coupled with numerous stakeholders with different agendas and consumers with different expectations.

The most common technique is simplifying complexity by using a partitioning approach.

Another way of simplifying a system is reducing the number of repetitive constituents.

Another technique could be moving an item from a large group of the clustered items but still, keep the relationship to preserve its core identity.

Moving with iterative steps, we can achieve some small results.

Simplicity touches almost every angle of transformation solutions, as these solutions can incredibly be complex.

The positive side of this negative result is that we fail cheap, and we fail quickly. Failing cheap and quickly don't make a big difference from a financial, commercial or project schedule perspectives.

Paradoxically, to create simplicity, one needs to deal with a lot of complexity, complications and sophisticated matters.

Creating simplicity for communication requires in-depth knowledge, flexible thinking, and demonstrated skills in articulation.

We must establish relationships that depict simplicity and efficiency with our stakeholders in our actions.

One of the effective ways to simplification for user-centricity is automating routine tasks and repetitive technology stacks. Automation can help standardise and simplify convoluted and repetitive tasks prone to human errors.

We need to have a specific mission to simplify the business and technology processes and make them user-centric.

Simplicity and clarity are closely related. An effective way of simplifying our processes and providing simplicity to the consumer is to think like the consumers.

Applying design thinking, combined with adopting agile methods for design, is one of the simplification approaches.

The digital trends, mobile culture and agile approaches made substantial changes in addressing the cumbersome specifications, especially concerning the users or consumers.

User stories are simple templates, including the functionalities, capabilities, and specifications from users or consumers point of view.

Refraining from convoluted phrases and instead, use of precise language and explicit statements are essential factors in simplifying communication.

When authoring a document, we must be sharp and to the point with clear statements.

Because of these known implications, it is critical to simplify governance framework, process and procedures for these initiatives.

One way of simplifying data is to clean it, remove duplications and errors. Reducing data sources and volumes, when needed, are also used to simplify and streamline data management processes.

Endless discussions may cloud the essential message; therefore, it is critical to control the presentation process and focus sharply on the essential points in our presentations.

We can provide simplified, clear and concise presentations without compromising the quality of content and effectiveness of the message.

Chapter 4: Manage Cost

Purpose

Arguably, the financial aspect of digital transformations can be the most important one. Even if we create a paragon of architecture with flawless designs, if the solution is economically not viable and it does not produce a compelling return on investment, it cannot be considered as successful.

Therefore, financial focus for digital transformation is mandatory and must be a priority objective. We need to consider the cost impact for every task and activity we undertake. A pragmatic architectural approach with priority setting is essential to keep the cost under control.

The purpose of this chapter is to provide a high-level view of digital cost and value propositions. Understanding the financial aspects makes valuable contributions to our digital intelligence.

Digital Cost Awareness

Everything in enterprise transformation generates substantial cost. There are known and hidden costs. It is relatively more comfortable to deal with the known costs; we can apply some logic and resources to address them. However, the real challenge is to deal with the hidden costs.

Hidden costs are the more significant part of the proverbial iceberg. When we are developing cost models for our digital transformation solutions, we need to always challenge the norms especially capital expenditure. For example, server, storage, and infrastructure costs for a simple development workload can be prohibitive therefore, we may consider moving these low priority, less sensitive workloads to inexpensive public cloud service offerings.

Even though financial teams manage the cost, the technical team need to find ways to make digital solutions inexpensive, affordable and lowering the cost gradually without compromising quality. Quality considerations are the critical requirements of digital transformation initiatives.

Quality and Cost Concerns

There is a common perception that making solutions cost-effective without compromising quality is not possible. The reason is that we must make a considerable number of trade-offs in the architecture and technical development phases. I partially agree with this statement. There are many challenges and factors to be considered to achieve this goal. Our approach makes a difference.

As transformation architects, we can contribute to reducing the solution costs by making trade-offs with a methodical and collaborative approach. For example, we can obtain collaborative input by bridging business and technology stakeholders. We can apply an agile approach and other innovative ways such as automation and standardisation to repetitive and resource-hungry components.

We can increase the quality of the solutions by applying professional diligence, architectural rigour, delivery agility, smart collaboration across multiple teams, and harvesting re-usable materials.

These principle-based and cost reduction approaches are critical to maintain and increase quality. Increasing quality can have a favourable effect on the overall financial viability of the solutions.

Bill of Materials

Simple yet a powerful impact on cost control is related to Bill of Materials in digital transformation programs. Bill of Materials refers to hardware, software, including licences, and services costs. As transformation architects, we can participate in cost model development proactively. For example, we can help develop a transformation solution Bill of Materials once we set the solution strategy and complete all high-level design artefacts.

Beware that there may be tremendous pressure from project managers and procurement staff to generate an upfront Bill of Materials due to demands of the project delivery lifecycle. However, we can point out that without an approved architecture and design, we cannot commence purchasing materials. Most of the times, it is not possible to obtain refunds for that expensive equipment purchased upfront without proper approval.

This assertive and straightforward action from our technical team members can save a considerable amount of funds to the enterprise modernisation and transformation programs or save wasting well controlled and tight budgets in this economic climate.

Unfortunately, I witnessed on several occasions, millions of dollars of materials purchased upfront and wasted due to changes in architecture and designs. They did not fit the purpose. This lesson learnt worth consideration.

Infrastructure and Maintenance Costs

There can be extensive infrastructure and maintenance costs associated with large data centres, server farms, mobile devices, storage units, data processing tools, analytics machines, and hosting in multi-Clouds.

These foundational infrastructure components are essential to make digital enterprise solutions viable. When we are developing our cost models, we ensure that they fit our capital expenditure goals at enterprise levels. There may be times that we can reuse some infrastructure components and tools. It always worth trying to procure internally first. This is a principle I developed in my extended teams and we saved substantial amount of money. Reusability is also environmentally friendly.

Another key consideration is single point of failures which may have a tremendous effect on the overall cost. Single failure or defect in a device or a group of devices serving the consumers via these high-end technology stacks can adversely affect the service levels hence could lead to high costs for the service providers.

Availability and Performance Costs

Availability and performance of the systems are the significant factors to address punitive service levels. One way to addressing these risks is the introduction of automation to service management.

Automated SLAs can detect low availability and poor performance. These automated SLAs trigger the rules and force the organisations breaching the agreements pay the contractually agreed penalties.

The downtime is the most critical factor for generating excessive penalties. The longer the systems are down, the higher the penalties. We need to take every measure from architectural standpoint to minimise system downtimes.

Our contribution to availability and performance by taking necessary measures can make a substantial difference in cost management of digital transformation programs. We discuss the implications of SLAs in the next section.

Service Level Agreements

Service downtime costs can be very high based on agreed rates and cause excessive penalties when accumulated for service-level breaches by organisations. Service Level breaches also have a strategic adverse effect on an organisation's product and services.

For example, downtimes in services or defects in products can result in poor client satisfaction. If we also look at from the consumer perspectives, they lose business due to service downtimes. It is a lose-lose scenario even though the consumer organisations are compensated with SLA penalties paid by the service providers.

We need to pay attention to the SLAs from the nascent stages of the digital solution lifecycle. The higher the quality of the solutions, the easier it is for SLAs to meet when the solutions are in production and the operational state. The rigour for quality in each phase can positively contribute to deal with SLA risks.

Some of the key considerations to address SLA issues could be autonomous condition monitoring and remote maintenance for the devices or systems in remote locations. Sending a technician to a remote location may take several hours of travel. However, fixing those units remotely can be done in minutes. One simple example in our projects that we applied was rebooting servers remotely. This simple task saved us considerable amount of time and money. It also helped us prevent SLA penalties.

There are specialist solutions regarding these trending techniques. It can be useful to assign automation and standardisation specialists for the design of these unique features in our digital solutions.

Service level management is particularly crucial in digital initiatives. To put this into a practical perspective, one of the biggest fears of the business executives is the impact of poor performance and availability problems damaging their organisations' client satisfaction and compromising business revenues in their transformed product and services.

To address the risks associated with this valid business concern, digital leaders need to pay special attention to SLA strategy, planning, design and implementation in an integrated way. A proactive and effective SLA management is one of the key areas where digital intelligence makes a real difference in cost management.

Digital Systems

Digital transformations are long journeys moving the enterprises from chaos to coherence. The transformation process includes every aspect of the enterprise. For the scope of this book, we focus on digital systems. Even though digital systems look only a tiny bit of an organisation in overarching enterprise, this domain by itself can be gigantic, especially for the large organisations.

Enterprise digital systems can include business IT processes, business data, business applications, IT infrastructure, and IT service delivery. These domains can even be more complicated with the addition of geographical factors such as adding multiple countries to the equation.

One of the essential workaround solutions for dealing with this complexity is to modernise these primary domains iteratively in parallel. Let's review the methodical approach that I present in the next section.

Methodical Approach to Cost Management

As transformation architects, we need to follow a methodical approach to manage the cost and contribute to the solution viability and profitability. Both a top-down and bottom-up approach must be applied depending on the needs.

At the top tier, we see the business and IT processes, and at the bottom tier, we see IT infrastructure. These two domains can independently be transformed using parallel activities. However, an integrated approach is essential as there can always be dependencies from multiple angles in both top-down and bottom-up approaches.

Once an organisation has an approved transformation strategy, then the digital leaders refine the strategy and convert it to clear architectural and technical formats. The strategy document is a critical artefact to bring all parties and stakeholders on the same page. Then we can identify the critical dependencies among these domains based on the short term, midterm and long-term considerations.

By using the strategy and considering the dependencies, we need to develop a high-level roadmap to inform the sponsoring executives. This roadmap can indicate the key outcomes, timelines and a ballpark cost for the overall modernisation and transformation activities. These indications initially can be at a very high level as there may be many factors affecting timelines, resources, and associated cost.

Once the roadmap for the digital transformation is set, we need to make a comprehensive viability assessment considering the current state of the scoped initiatives, their indicative future state and the strategies to reach the end state. This viability assessment must include key risks, constraints, and dependencies. The viability assessment can be the most informative tool a digital solution lead can provide to the sponsoring executives to make informed decisions.

After review and approval of the viability assessment, we delve into collecting the high-level requirements of the solutions based on the domains we mentioned earlier. As dealing with the requirements of those domains can be daunting, we can delegate the requirements collection process with the domain and program architects, technical specialists, and business analysts based on their skills set relevant to the types of requirements.

In this phase, the role of the transformation architect is to coordinate and facilitate the requirements management team, which can consist of multiple solution architects, technical specialists, and business analysts.

After requirements are collected and analysed at a reasonable amount, the next important activity is to prioritise the requirements based on business impact. We need to develop criteria to prioritise the requirements based on factors depicted in the strategy and roadmap documents, as well as the financial and business priorities set by the sponsoring executives.

Following this methodical yet straightforward approach, we can be on top of issues and contribute to the control of cost. Reducing cost can also increase the financial viability of the digital solution.

Besides we need to introduce innovation continuously, as a cost reduction enabler, as it can be the dominant player for overall cost management in complex digital environments. We cover the innovation in a separate chapter subsequently due to its significance in cost management and return on investment.

Chapter Summary and Take Away Points

Even if we create a paragon of architecture with flawless designs, if the solution is economically not viable and it does not produce a compelling return on investment, it cannot be considered as successful.

Everything in enterprise transformation generates substantial cost. There are known and hidden costs. Hidden costs are the more significant part of the proverbial iceberg.

Even though financial teams manage the cost, the technical team need to find ways to make digital solutions inexpensive, affordable and lowering the cost gradually without compromising quality.

Beware that there may be tremendous pressure from project managers and procurement staff to generate an upfront Bill of Materials due to demands of the project delivery lifecycle.

Automated SLAs can detect low availability and poor performance. These automated SLAs trigger the rules and force the organisations breaching the agreements pay the contractually agreed penalties.

We need to pay attention to the SLAs from the nascent stages of the digital solution lifecycle. The higher the quality of the solutions, the easier it is for SLAs to meet when the solutions are in production and the operational state.

Enterprise digital systems can include business IT processes, business data, business applications, IT infrastructure, and IT service delivery. These domains can even be more complicated with the addition of geographical factors such as adding multiple countries to the equation.

Chapter 5: Innovate & Invent

Purpose

I attempt to reflect upon my observations and thoughts on how transformation architects can use innovative and inventive approach coupled with collaborative principles of fusion-focused approach to initiate, empower, and deliver enterprise modernisation and digital transformation goals.

In this chapter, we aim to understand the importance of innovative and inventive intelligence as an empowering factor for the success of modernisation and digital transformation.

We need to reach a common understanding of the innovative and inventive thinking process in this practical context. The subsequent sections lay out the key points.

Innovation and Invention

We can define innovative and inventive thinking in different terms based on the type of work, professions, industry, and other backgrounds relate to our digital goals.

In this book, my definition of innovative and inventive thinking is the use of creativity for generating novel ideas, new methods, new approaches, new techniques, new processes, and new tools or improve the current environment to gain insights, add compelling business value, reduce unnecessary costs, and increase desired revenue by focussing on return on investment from our digital transformation endeavours.

Innovation and invention relate to novelty, improvement, iterations for ongoing steady progress. Innovative and inventive thinking generates novel ideas, focuses on improving ideas, and strives for making continuous iterative progress. To this end, innovative and inventive thinking can use agile delivery principles to reach their goals. Innovative and inventive thinking must be practical rather than theoretical. They need to add immediate value.

Innovative and inventive thinking feeds the culture and is a critical aspect of a modernising ecosystem in transforming organisations for digital goals. Enterprise cultures embracing innovative and inventive thinking approaches can naturally renew themselves to survive and thrive in fluctuating conditions, which are typical situations in modernising and transforming enterprises. These enterprises extend to the next generations with constant progress, renewed image, improved services, and stronger capabilities.

Innovation, inventions, technical excellence, and agility are interrelated and go hand in hand. Innovative and inventive thinking ignites technical excellence, and technical excellence can be empowered by agility. Therefore, as digital transformation architects, we must be natural innovators and inventors producing results in agility.

We need to practice innovative and inventive thinking in all walks of our professional life and motivate people around us. Now, let's attempt to find some practical ways to generate inventive and innovative intelligence for our digital transformation goals.

Thinking Modes

Innovation and invention require multiple modes of thinking differently. Traditionally, most of us think vertically, linearly or in binary. We usually use vertical and linear types of thinking for problem-solving.

Applying practical logic coupled with streamlining our thoughts aligned with digital goals are some fundamentals approaches in this type of thinking mode. Linear thinking goes deep down, layer by layer, and in a sequential and logical manner.

There are times we may need to use binary thinking to assess and validate some immediate situations. Binary thinking consists of simple terms such as yes or no, black and white, good or bad. This type of thinking can be useful in a certain context however it has its limitations for qualitative assessment requirements.

As opposed to vertical thinking, horizontal thinking covering more breadth rather than depth aims to generate unpredictable ideas by breaking out the rigid thought patterns. By using horizontal thinking, we challenge the assumptions posed in our situations. In this type of thinking mode, we look for alternatives and go beyond the ordinary leading to radical creative solutions.

We can apply horizontal thinking to create innovative and inventive ideas in our digital transformation pursuits. There are different techniques that we can leverage horizontal thinking.

Some commonly used techniques for horizontal thinking are randomisations, distortions, reversals, exaggerations, metaphors, analogies, dreaming, theme mining, questioning the norms, and creating contradictions. Using these techniques opens new opportunities for our creativity.

One of the practical techniques to generate innovative and inventive ideas is to use traditional mind mapping. We can articulate our thoughts using representative maps on paper or a whiteboard.

We can also use other visual representations, such as drawing pictures on a whiteboard while explaining abstract ideas. We can visualise abstract ideas better by looking at the drawing as the proverbial a single picture can tell a thousand words.

Creating Innovation and Invention Culture

Many digitally transforming enterprises attempt to create an innovation and invention culture embedded in their modernising ecosystem. As transformation architects, we are the catalyst for the formation and maintenance of this empowering culture.

With the support of the technical team members of our digitally transforming ecosystem, we continually challenge the status quo. Our team members embrace changes and challenges by seeing the transformation at first hand in these cultures.

People collaborate better in cultures embracing innovative and inventive ideas. They see themselves with the changing conditions in new positions. They do not resist as they know that change can be useful for them.

In these enriching cultures, we create excellence centres or ideation labs for people to try new ideas. We need to perform ongoing trials and errors to create and test our compelling ideas. We may fail at times, but they fail quickly and come back to reality with improved knowledge. We must see the failing tests as new definitions.

Harnessing and driving creative thinking result in new cultures. As digital transformation architects, we need to cultivate the transforming culture and inspire our team members. The best way for to ignite innovation and invention for inspiration is to be a role model for our team members. We need to encourage the team members to innovate, invent and reward them for their achievements.

In transforming organisations, innovation and invention become habitual. Our team members strive for excellence by creating new ideas in their day to day tasks. No one is called weird names or with other judgemental adjectives. Instead, new ideas are welcomed, praised, and even awarded in different ways.

In our evidently transforming environments, our team members embrace constant change and new ideas, even if these challenges can be painful at times. We learn how to turn the pain to pleasure with the rewarding results of evident transformations.

Metaphorically, innovation is like air and water for our survival. In addition to survival, we need to use innovative and inventive thinking for thriving. We not only need to create innovations and inventions at a personal level but also through collaboration with the immediate teams and extended teams.

In our transforming environments, we must keep asking how to deliver innovative and inventive experiences moment by moment continuously. This is a cultural shift that we all need to embrace for collective success.

Design Thinking

One of the methods we can use to maintain an innovative and inventive culture can be achieved by use of the design thinking practice. This can take place daily in the team interactions.

Design thinking allows the team to be intuitive and logical at the same time. Design thinking enables team members to be more creative to recognise new patterns. We apply design thinking to our digital transformation activities at all times.

As design thinking is closely associated with the agile approach, the design thinking professionals progress their ideas iteratively. Enterprise modernisation and digital transformation initiatives require the adoption of design thinking to its core culture. Design thinking can result in a creative cultural shift to support our digital transformation goals.

Growth Mindset

We need to have a growth mindset to ignite innovation and invention in our transforming ecosystem. We must help our team members with a fixed mindset to convert to a growth mindset.

We know that a growth mindset can lead to innovative and inventive solutions, it must be a build-in characteristic in the personalities of people in the transforming ecosystem.

As transformation architects, we must lead to a mindset shift in immediate and extended teams. We must hold a positive 'can do' attitude for any challenges we come across in our transforming environments.

We must also have customer-centric mindset and put ourselves in customers' shoes with strong empathy. Applying design thinking techniques, we can develop empathy maps which can enable us to think like our customers. The mindset based on empathy is part of the design thinking practice and can be embedded to our culture.

Co-creation

To ignite innovation and invention culture, we need to consider market conditions and the needs of our clients. These challenging conditions can help us generate new ideas. Listening to our clients carefully and collaborating with them can help us focus on innovative thinking and enable us to invent novel solutions.

Many innovations and inventions can be co-created with clients. Co-creation can be seen as a win-win situation for both the service providers and their consumers.

A client-centric innovation and invention approach can be invaluable for digital transformation goals. We can link client concerns, requirements, expectations, and aspirations to our organisation's capabilities then define the focus areas for innovation and invention agendas to enable our digital transformation goals to address client needs.

Innovation and Invention Roadblocks

There can be many visible and invisible roadblocks to creating innovation and inventions; therefore, it is critical to recognise potential roadblocks.

The roadblocks can be in various shapes and forms from various angles. One of the main roadblocks can be keeping the status quo and silos. Traditional enterprises and business processes usually tend to maintain the status quo isolated from other entities of the enterprise. There may be strong resistance to change and amalgamation in these cultures.

Many organisations nowadays recognise the importance of innovative and inventive thinking to achieve transformation goals. However, there may be unknown fears and resistance towards novelties by some team members who may have hidden or differing agendas to the core values. These variances in team goals may constitute political, economic, commercial and cultural implications,

As digital transformation architects, we must be alert and recognise team member who may have differing agendas and intentionally or unintentionally try to sabotage innovative and inventive thinking in our transformation goals. Even though these people with a negative mindset may be in the minority, they still can have a tremendous adverse impact on desired progress.

One way of dealing with resisting people is to be transparent to them and have a close face to face conversations. We must find ways to engage those types of team members and show the value and benefit of new ideas which can benefit them. If those people can see the value for themselves, then they can be converted to our supporters of transformation goals. The critical point is engaging them and encouraging them to think positively.

The business as usual mentality can be a roadblock for new ideas. Our team members dealing with the business as usual aspect all the time create a comfort zone with habitual behaviour. The transformation activities can be seen as disruptors of their comfort zones. More importantly, tired employees can hardly have any interest in innovation and inventions as they cannot see the immediate need.

One of the workaround solutions can be to separate new and old business as usual as two different departments. However, we must find some collaborative ways to bridge them.

Of course, business, as usual, is essential for the organisation to continue its current function but these organisations also need innovation and invention for transforming to the digital world with new insights, market competitiveness, and revenue generation.

It is usually recommended that the modernisation and digital transformation programs can be kept separate from the business as usual practices to prevent any adverse effect of traditional thinking; however, we must integrate them in a way to prevent the undesirable effects of the old thinking models.

We also need to watch out cumbersome business processes which can be deterrent factors for innovation and invention goals for transforming environments. Activities may take too long to complete, and the team members struggle to cope with the difficulties for dealing with archaic processes. We highlighted the importance of simplifying the processes in previous chapter.

Chapter Summary and Take Away Points

We can define innovative and inventive thinking as the use of creativity for generating novel ideas, new methods, new approaches, new techniques, new processes, and new tools or improve the current environment to gain insights, add compelling business value, reduce unnecessary costs, and increase desired revenue by focussing on return on investment from our digital transformation endeavours.

Innovation and invention require multiple modes of thinking differently.

Binary thinking consists of simple terms such as yes or no, black and white, good or bad. This type of thinking can be useful in a certain context however it has its limitations for qualitative assessment requirements.

Some commonly used techniques for horizontal thinking are randomisations, distortions, reversals, exaggerations, metaphors, analogies, dreaming, theme mining, questioning the norms, and creating contradictions. Using these techniques opens new opportunities for our creativity.

In transforming organisations, innovation and invention become habitual. Our team members strive for excellence by creating new ideas in their day to day tasks. No one is called weird names or with other judgemental adjectives.

Design thinking allows the team to be intuitive and logical at the same time. Design thinking enables team members to be more creative to recognise new patterns. We apply design thinking to our digital transformation activities at all times.

We must also have customer-centric mindset and put ourselves in customers' shoes with strong empathy.

Many innovations and inventions can be co-created with clients. Co-creation can be seen as a win-win situation for both the service providers and their consumers.

One way of dealing with resisting people is to be transparent to them and have a close face to face conversations. We must find ways to engage those types of team members and show the value and benefit of new ideas which can benefit them.

One of the workaround solutions can be to separate new and old business as usual as two different departments. However, we must find some collaborative ways to bridge them.

We also need to watch out cumbersome business processes which can be deterrent factors for innovation and invention goals for transforming environments.

Chapter 6: Accelerate Delivery

Purpose

Accelerating our solution delivery with using agile approach is the next critical pillar in our digital transformation method. As transformation architects, in this era, we must be nimble, agile and think on our feet at all times.

Approaching our goals with agility provides us with a competitive advantage in our organisation and can help us to be influential, credible, competitive, and productive in our modernisation and transformation engagements.

We need to be mindful that our business teams and customers expect us to act in agility. As transformation architects, we need to embrace agile delivery and make it as part of our transforming culture. We need to delve into details on how to develop an agile culture to accelerate our digital transformation delivery. Let's start with agile thinking and acting.

Agile Thinking and Acting

In this day and age, agile thinking and acting are essential attributes for the transformation architects striving to architect their digital transformation. We cannot afford slow thinking and acting in these rapidly changing environments.

By using agile thinking and rapid actions, we can ask empowering questions by comparing and contrasting at all times. For example, we keep asking how we can make our IT footprint more intuitive, responsive, and nimble day today whilst remaining a reliable service offering.

This type of thinking mode is a foundational requirement of our modernisation and digital transformation initiatives. Whist dealing with legacy IT footprint to understand it in an agile manner, we also need to have the vision of well-functioning solutions and put our energies on rapid-paced iterative modernisation and digital transformation initiatives. Dealing with opposing situations requires a fine balance.

It is not feasible to undertake successful digital initiatives with an old way of thinking and using old methods. As this became a reality, many organisations embraced agility and matured in delivering rapidly.

We know that agility is a particular concern for modernisation and digital transformations as consumer demands are increasing based on fast-paced delivery requirements. In order to meet the challenges of these rapid changes and growing demands, we need to apply agile thinking and acting to our digital transformation pursuits. Let's touch the importance of speed for market advantage.

Speed to Market

Speed to market is one of the most fundamental requirements of digital transformation initiatives. We can generate revenues only by acting very quickly in this competitive world.

To this end, fast delivery using agile approaches became the new norm in transforming enterprises. Our products are expected to be released faster than they were in the past. Security updates and bug fixes are required more frequently.

Speed to market affects all aspects of the digital enterprise and creates many challenges for the service providers. This challenge makes it imperative to act, behave, and approach in agility to stay competitive in the market.

Promoting Accelerated Delivery

Accelerated delivery is essential to achieve our digital transformation goals. However, there may be some resistance to accelerated approaches in some traditionally slow-acting businesses.

The good news is that promoting accelerated delivery to many business stakeholders nowadays can be reasonably easy due to its benefits and compelling business value in the competitive market place.

As a positive aspect, accelerated delivery is a particular interest to the new generations as they grow with agility in all walks of life. However, the older generation still has a sentimental attachment to traditional approaches such as using waterfall methods for their projects.

There appears to be some comfort zone created for using waterfall methods in traditional organisations. Therefore, we need to find some creative ways and demonstrate compelling benefits to promote agile to those resisting it and particularly to older generations.

Quality Perceptions for Fast Delivery

There is a common perception that fast delivery methods such as agile approach can cut things short hence may reduce the quality; however, this is not true. Projects applying agile approaches increase the quality with the progressive and iterative approaches checking quality more frequently in every iteration and milestone.

We must articulate the benefits and compelling reasons to use the agile approach, especially for modernisations programs leading to digital transformations. It is not feasible to wait and see the end of a gigantic digital transformation project. There are always many unknowns; hence, it is not possible to see the end product without experimentation and constant trial and errors in smaller scales.

An accelerated delivery method using an agile approach allows the team members to test their ideas quickly and iteratively. If they fail, they fail quickly and cheaply without costing lots of funds to the initiatives.

The business value gained by accelerated delivery methods needs to be understood well and needs to be embedded in the culture of the organisations striving for digital transformation goals. We can be the catalyst for conveying the message and making the necessary cultural adjustments effectively in our architecting teams.

As digital transformation architects, we must be motivators and ignite accelerated delivery in all of our digital transformation initiatives. As we are technically capable and business-focused, we need to show the value and share our knowledge and views with our technical team members and business stakeholders.

As a role model architects, we can provide ongoing feedback and architectural support to the scrum teams striving for accelerated delivery using agile approaches. Transformation architects must be agile champions to accelerate delivery for digital transformation goals.

Roles and Responsibilities for Accelerated Delivery

Accelerated delivery for digital transformations requires multiple roles and responsibilities. An accelerated delivery approach requires using agile methods across multiple teams called scrum teams. These teams work collaboratively and in an integrated way.

The most common roles in agile teams are the scrum master, the product owner, and the scrum team member. As transformation architects, we can perform the role of the product owner for digital transformation programs using agile scrums. As we are architecting the digital solutions, we are in an excellent position to own the digital product or services that we are architecting.

As product owners, we can set the acceptance criteria for a digital product or service in the allocated transformation sprint. Providing an effective acceptance criterion can lead the team to think in the right direction. Our leadership and ownership of digital products are paramount for the success of accelerated delivery.

We can also serve as a scrum master. The scrum master role requires us to provide day to day guidance on developing agile user stories, clearing backlogs, running stand-up meetings, and designing iterative solutions for digital transformation initiatives. This is a lead architecting role for accelerated delivery.

Agile Awareness for Accelerated Delivery

Agile awareness for digital transformation initiatives requires developing quick mental models on how technology users interact with their solution in each iteration. To maintain accelerated delivery, we need to apply agile principles. For example, using these agile principles we can clear our transformation backlogs in the most efficient ways. Clearing our backlogs rapidly and efficiently is essential for accelerated delivery.

In order to deliver with speed, we need to prioritise our backlogs. With our rapid action-oriented approach, we can clear the backlogs quickly in priority orders. Furthermore, we can use rewards and recognise the high achievers' effort and contributions for clearing the backlogs in the most effective and innovative ways.

In many organisations, due to valid reasons, developing architecture and designs create fear for the sponsors. The main reason for this is that architecture involves things that are hard to change later.

However, this doesn't mean we cannot apply an accelerated approach to architecture. Our awareness of accelerated delivery and applying it at a constant basis can add great value to complete our architectural and design activities.

There is a massive trend to use accelerated delivery methods for developing architectural and design solutions for digital transformation initiatives.

To address the fear of architecture and designs, I introduce the term pragmatic architecture in fast-paced modernisations and digital transformation initiatives in my recent projects. Let's discuss the importance and necessity of using a pragmatic architecting approach.

Pragmatic Architecting Approach

We know that predicting the future is very hard; therefore, creating an upfront paragon of architecture is not practical. To this end, as transformation architects, we must take a pragmatic approach to architecture development when engaged in enterprise modernisation and digital transformation programs.

Pragmatism negates perfectionism. The notion of perfection equates to failure in fast-paced digital transformation programs. We cannot afford the use of monolithic waterfall methods for perfecting and developing architectures and designs for many months and even years. This slow approach is not sustainable and does not suit the demands of digital transformation goals.

Taking extended times is not feasible in this digital age any more. Consumers expect product and services much quicker than old times. Our profitability depends on our speed to market. Therefore, a pragmatic and accelerated approach to architecture and design is essential for successful digital transformation initiatives.

To enable accelerated delivery for architecting, an iterative approach to architecture can be the most effective investment in the earlier stages of the digital transformation. We can see the architecture development like product development. The incremental and iterative approach can speed up the architectural process and improve the quality of architecting based on the minimally viable product development approach.

Another way of accelerated pragmatic approach is to use a single domain and apply the learnings to the next domains. This single domain approach allows us progress incrementally with iterative approach. This approach can help us progress with confidence depicting a well-managed risk profile.

Accelerated Development

After architecture and design, another big topic and concern in digital transformation initiatives is software or application development. Development activities are time-consuming and can be very costly.

As we all know, by using waterfall methods developing a software product used take months and years in the past. Nowadays, our consumers cannot wait this long any more. The solution to accelerated development phase is applying an agile approach to software development. Fortunately, agile methods are more suited to the development areas and broadly accepted by modern developers.

There are many evolving agile methods to support different kinds of software development processes. Fortunately, many software developers understand the importance and embrace agile methods. These developers can see the results much more quickly by accelerating the delivery for consumer and market demands.

Use of evolving methods such as DevOps is also prime considerations for accelerating delivery of software development products for substantial digital transformation initiatives. DevOps brings the software development and infrastructure support operations teams together in an integrated way. The developers don't have to concern about the infrastructure issues any more. Applying DevOps practice to digital transformation initiatives can speed up the delivery of software products for timely consumption.

As digital transformation architects, we can encourage rapid application development and deployment of flexible solutions using appropriate agile methods and DevOps principles in our organisation.

We need to be mindful that speedy time-to-market for digital products is a competitive differentiator in this day and age. The rapid software development solutions for market demands can also delight our clients and increase their confidence in our products and services.

Accelerate Delivery with Automation and Standardisation

Enterprise modernisation goals leading to digital transformation for our services and delivering our products fast to market requires substantial automation and standardisation activities. We need to leverage the benefits of automation and standardisation for accelerated delivery.

Principally, agile methods have a particular focus on automation and standardisation hence mandates applying them as much as possible in every scrum. It is well known that both automation and standardisation can enable simplifying and speeding up processes to meet consumption demands.

As we understand the value of automation and standardisation for increasing the quality of our products and services, we need to encourage our teams to leverage these two enablers in our digital transformation solutions. Many teams would embrace both automation and standardisation as the value is quite clear and compelling.

Applying automation and standardisation to our digital transformation objectives, we can reduce the number of resources required to maintain manual and tedious tasks. It is evident that computers can manage repetitive tasks much more effectively than human beings.

Automation and standardisation can address human errors and resolve potential errors quickly. Enterprises embracing accelerated delivery and agile cultures do not resist automation and standardisation; in fact, they leverage these critical capabilities for the success of their digital transformation goals.

By encouraging our domain architects, solutions designers, subject matter experts, and technical specialists to automate and standardise as much as possible, we can enable these valuable resources to participate in more value-adding roles rather than performing repetitive and boring tasks that computers can undertake.

Team members focusing on stimulating and high-value items also tend to create more innovative solutions to empower enterprise modernisation and digital transformation progress.

Accelerate Delivery by Breaking Silos

Accelerated delivery for digital transformations requires removing silos in enterprises. What I mean by silos are having isolated departments and teams without being integrated into other relevant departments and teams in the organisation. This undesirable separation is unnecessary and can be unproductive.

Silos in organisations are proven to slow the whole enterprise modernisation and digital transformation lifecycle, including architecture, design, development, deployment, marketing, and selling products and services.

A siloed culture can also impact the quality of the products due to a lack of integrated views. Enterprise departments in silos may not know each other's progress and cause some duplicate of works or rework. They may not produce a single integrated product or services to the consumers and delay the delivery pace.

Another undesirable implication of having silos is that some departments in these traditional settings in the same organisations even compete with each other. Internal competition is the worst enemy which can slow down and destroy any digital transformation goals and objectives.

Leveraging our accelerated delivery mindset, we can move from silos to a flatter structure to resolve the issues of isolated and hierarchical structures in large organisations. By leveraging the agile principles, we can pay special attention to collaboration, co-locations, and face to face teamwork rather than having silos and hierarchies in our organisations, leading to faster delivery for digital transformation product and services.

Maintaining accelerated delivery mindset, we continuously need to deal with aging culture to prevent it to speedy delivery of our digital transformation goals. In short, we need to break silos for accelerated delivery. Instead of coming above, we can create flat structures, resulting in collaborative self-managing teams with many domain experts as peers for accelerated delivery.

Accelerate Delivery by Prioritising Backlogs

Inevitably, digital transformation initiatives can have gigantic backlogs. Dealing with accumulated digital transformation backlogs can be very challenging and discouraging for accelerated delivery.

However, our agile awareness mandating prioritisation can serve well in clearing backlogs efficiently and rapidly. Maintaining backlogs in agile methods is systemic and embedded in the culture. As digital transformation architects in scrums, we can make day to day management of backlogs in priority order, a habit.

Even if we perform the role of a scrum master or a product owner, we need to keep the team members accountable for their backlog items. We can help the team manage their assigned backlogs items in priority order effectively.

We cannot emphasise enough that as transformation architects, we must focus on the priority items in the digital transformation backlogs based on precise priority orders set by our transformation strategy and aligned with our delivery goals and objectives.

Leveraging this priority approach day to day and encouraging our team members to do so, our transformation backlogs can run efficiently and productively. We know that backlog management is a critical factor for accelerated delivery of our digital transformation sprints. We keep sprinting with prioritised acceleration.

Accelerate Delivery with Minimum Viable Product

One of the critical aspects of accelerated delivery is the creation of a minimum viable product using agile principles. We practice this acceleration using the well-recognised sprint concept.

A sprint is the shortest time bombed duration to create the minimum viable product. A sprint duration usually a two to three-week period. This limited-time speeds up delivery and encourages the team to focus on the priority items to create the minimum viable product.

Consumer expectations, financial constraints, resource issues, and business priorities all have an impact on setting priorities to clear our digital transformation backlogs to create minimum viable products for our consumers.

This agile principle of creating a minimum viable product can help us set the priorities for value creation for digital transformation goals aiming to delight our clients for accelerated delivery of our services progressively.

Accelerate Delivery with Constant Change

Accelerated delivery mandates dealing with constant change. Change management is a vital aspect of enterprise modernisation and digital transformation initiatives.

For the entire digital transformation team, embracing change is critical to be successful with accelerated delivery. Adapting to constant change can help us keep the momentum for accelerated delivery.

Managing every user story, clearing a backlog item on a timely basis, and running a sprint is all about accelerating delivery with constant change. Dealing with this constant change requires flexibility and agility in designing, developing and implementing rapid solutions for our customers.

To this end, digital transformation architects and the architecting team members engaged in accelerated delivery processes adapt to the constant change. They become the change agents. Success of our digital transformation initiatives depends on change-oriented accelerated delivery.

Accelerate Delivery by Failing Rapidly, Early, and Cheaply

As we keep highlighting throughout this book, one of the benefits of using accelerated approach comes from moving in small steps quickly. In other words, we tackle solutions in smaller chunks with agility.

Accelerated delivery empowered by an agile approach mandates the principles of the fail fast, fail early, and fail cheaply. These principles are fundamental success factors for our modernisation and digital transformation goals.

Of course, we don't fail for the sake of failure. No one enjoys failure, but it is beneficial to fail earlier than later to keep the cost of failure low and be successful in the long run using the lessons learnt from smaller failures. Learning from failures and redefining success is a crucial agile intelligence attribute for digital transformation architects and architecting team members.

Even though we call it 'fail fast', realistically it refers to ongoing experimentation with constant trial and errors leading to further intelligence and learning to deal with unknowns in an accelerated, effective, and productive way.

Learnings from our iterative and incremental experimentations constitute desired progress for designing, developing, and implementing complex solutions for our enterprise modernisation and digital transformation goals.

Accelerated Cost Management

Accelerated delivery mandates cost awareness. In business, every resource and effort constitute a cost. Accelerated delivery help us reduce cost in many ways.

As applying accelerated delivery in our architecture and design works, we contribute to reducing cost of delivery for our digital transformation initiatives. We are cost-aware architects. We know how to reduce cost with our intelligent decisions affecting overall transformation.

By delivering rapidly and in agility, we make our projects profitable and contribute to generate more revenue from accelerated delivery. We focus on increasing efficiencies via standardisation and automation lowering traditional costs as part of our modern digital strategy.

Accelerated delivery is a cost-focused and revenue-generating approach. We can manage costs better and generate more revenue by adopting agile principles in high impact tasks and solution development activities in modernisation and digital transformation solutions.

Through incremental progress, prioritised backlog management, speedy iterative delivery through sprints, we can prevent the cost of failure for big chunks of work items and more importantly, we can turn the costs into revenues.

As digital transformation architects and architecting team members, we are capable of turning costs to investment. With a strong vision, innovative approaches, and agile delivery capabilities, the costs incurred from our initiatives can be an investment rather than cost.

Sponsoring executives for digital transformation initiatives are aware that investment on visionary and well-performing digital leaders like us can generate new businesses and bring substantial revenues in modernisation and digital transformation initiatives with our contributions both at tactical and strategic levels.

Chapter Summary and Take Away Points

As transformation architects, we need to embrace agile delivery and make it as part of our transforming culture.

Whist dealing with legacy IT footprint to understand it in an agile manner, we also need to have the vision of well-functioning solutions and put our energies on rapid-paced iterative modernisation and digital transformation initiatives.

Speed to market is one of the most fundamental requirements of digital transformation initiatives. We can generate revenues only by acting very quickly in this competitive world.

There appears to be some comfort zone created for using waterfall methods in traditional organisations.

Accelerated delivery for digital transformations requires multiple roles and responsibilities.

The most common roles in agile teams are the scrum master, the product owner, and the scrum team member.

Providing an effective acceptance criterion can lead the team to think in the right direction.

To address the fear of architecture and designs, we can apply pragmatic architecture in fast-paced modernisations and digital transformation initiatives in our programs.

Pragmatism negates perfectionism. The notion of perfection equates to failure in fast-paced digital transformation programs.

Taking extended times is not feasible in this digital age any more.

We can see the architecture development like product development.

Use of evolving methods such as DevOps is also prime considerations for accelerating delivery of software development products for substantial digital transformation initiatives.

Applying automation and standardisation to our digital transformation objectives, we can reduce the number of resources required to maintain manual and tedious tasks.

Accelerated delivery for digital transformations requires removing silos in enterprises. A siloed culture can also impact the quality of the products due to a lack of integrated views.

Another undesirable implication of having silos is that some departments in these traditional settings in the same organisations even compete with each other.

We cannot emphasise enough that as transformation architects, we must focus on the priority items in the digital transformation backlogs based on precise priority orders set by our transformation strategy and aligned with our delivery goals and objectives.

A sprint is the shortest time bombed duration to create the minimum viable product. A sprint duration usually a two to three-week period. This limited-time speeds up delivery and encourages the team to focus on the priority items to create the minimum viable product.

Accelerated delivery empowered by an agile approach mandates the principles of the fail fast, fail early, and fail cheaply.

By delivering rapidly and in agility, we make our projects profitable and contribute to generate more revenue from accelerated delivery.

Through incremental progress, prioritised backlog management, speedy iterative delivery through sprints, we can prevent the cost of failure for big chunks of work items and more importantly, we can turn the costs into revenues.

Chapter 7: Grow with Collaboration

Purpose

As digital transformation architects and architecting team members, we certainly need to take leverage of collaborative intelligence across the enterprise and beyond to create a competitive advantage in our digital transformation pursuits.

In this section, we cover the importance of collaboration from a productivity angle in the modernising and digitally transforming enterprise. Let's start with the meaning of collaboration in our desired context.

Meaning of Collaboration

We know that the term collaboration is overused and loses its significance, especially with the emergence of internet technologies. People keep saying collaborative or collaboration tools, especially in a social media context.

In its true meaning, collaboration refers to a team of people working together for mutual goals to achieve successful and synergetic outcomes. The team, mutual goals, and synergetic outcomes are essential entities of this simple framework. Our focus is, of course, on the work aspect of the collaboration rather than entertainment or hobbies.

Collaboration may take place in different modes and formats. One example is two or more people sharing ideas for a project plan. At a basic level, people may also collaborate by writing using various documentation tools such as Box, Google docs, or network version of Microsoft Office products.

There are also emerging tools mainly used in mobile settings. These mobility tools are widespread in agile methods. To give an idea, some of these tools are Slack, Trello, Twitter, Facebook Messenger, and many more.

Most of us tout social media tools as practical, useful, and highly valuable for collaboration purposes. However, when we carefully examine these tools, we can see that they are more information-sharing tools rather than actual collaboration tools. From my experience, the most productive and impactful collaboration tools are face to face meetings, telephone, and video conferencing.

Collaboration is essential to create synergy in digital transformation teams. As digital transformation architects, we collaborate widely and productively. We also motivate our team members to collaborate effectively and efficiently by pointing out the common goals and making them compelling for collaboration. Related to collaboration, we need to understand the powerful metaphor of fusion.

Collaborative Intelligence with Fusion

We can consider fusion an empowering attribute for digital transformation architects and the architecting team members. The term fusion refers to joining different things with different attributes or functions together to create a single new entity or form. The notion of fusion relates to concepts such as integration, blending, merging, amalgamation, synergy, and bonding.

Fusion is closely related to collaboration from several angles. Fusion is a type of collaboration designed for specific and advanced missions. Fusion principles suit the goals of transformation progress in an enterprise.

Fusion principles aim to bring individuals from various backgrounds, small groups with different purposes, various teams with differing capabilities, communities of practices with different missions under a single umbrella for serving a joint mission.

Fusion is the most advanced and effective type of collaboration especially required for complex and complicated modernisation initiatives with unique goals and market focus. Creating fusion-based collaboration can be very challenging. As digital transformation architects, with extensive technical and people skills and experiences, we can create fusion-based collaboration for our digital transformation goals.

Fusion can also refer to integrating old systems, tools, and processes and creating new systems. This transformative approach is a critical factor for enterprise modernisation and digital transformation goals. From an awareness perspective, we need to understand the significance of fusion principles and apply them to help our organisations to modernise the enterprise effectively.

There are different ways to enable fusion in an organisation. As transformation architects, we usually take responsibility to initiate fusion in our immediate and extended teams in the digital transformation initiatives.

We must be passionate about achieving our digital goals using fusion principles. We don't wait for fusion to happen by itself. We know that nothing can happen by itself. Naturally, someone with leadership and architectural skills must initiate it. This action-oriented focus on fusion is one of the outstanding characteristics of strategic transformation architects, who are typically extrovert people.

Once we initiate fusion and invite our collaborators to structured activities, then the process is maintained with necessary communication and engagement rules. Effective communication is a critical enabler of fusion goals. Depending on the medium, both verbal and written communication types are essential for fusion to happen.

Fusion for co-located teams are usually conducted on face to face and can primarily be dynamic in delivery. However, geographically distant teams usually use video conferencing, telephone, chat programs, email or some agile collaboration tools.

In remote teams, written communication is critical. Written communications can create some challenges, such as a careless piece of writing may cause some offence and kill the spirit of collaboration. Therefore, as transformation architects, we play an essential role in facilitating these types of communication by moderating communication channels delicately.

After we initiate and enable fusion goals, we need to maintain the desired outcomes. We can create the necessary process and procedures to maintain collaborative activities. Effective use of our strategic leadership skills is mandatory to achieve fusion goals in modernisation and digital transformation initiatives.

Even though we set the initial team and processes to support the team activities, it is also the responsibilities of other team members to contribute to the goals set by our collaborative plans. To this end, as transformation architects, we also take the role of motivators to keep the transformation team inspired by showing their impactful vision and strategic goals.

By focusing on productive fusion at various levels, we leverage insights from cross-functional teams and community of practices to create differentiated value propositions for our modernisation and digital transformation goals.

By undertaking many tasks to initiate and maintain fusion, we keep repeating these activities multiple times with multiple teams and integrate these teams to aggregate more intensive collaboration.

The magic of fusion starts with these repetitions. Successful repetitions make ripple effects for more success. In a relatively short time frame, these teams can create a collaborative culture based on fusion principles aligned with the organisation's ecosystem and strategic goals.

This collaborative culture at work can be invaluable. When collaborative culture starts flourishing using fusion-based collaboration, a desirable phenomenon called innovation happens naturally.

Collaboration and innovation are tightly coupled processes, as we mentioned in previous chapters. As a critical subject, it is time to discuss diversity within collaboration and fusion context.

Diversity for Collaboration

The power of connected people from diverse backgrounds for the same goal generates new ideas and insights. Some of these ideas and insights may touch people from different angles and further motivate them even to take more responsibilities in this transforming ecosystem.

With the ignition of the initial strategic technical leadership, this shift causes the emergence of new technical leaders in modernising enterprises. Innovation generates collaborative culture and can be highly desirable for creating new business and growing established businesses by modernising the enterprise leading to desired digital transformation goals. Innovation is one of the exciting results provided by a collaborative culture with diversity, inclusiveness and implementation of fusion approach.

Diversity oriented magical aspect of fusion and collaboration leading to innovation is an ideal situation for transforming the enterprise. As transformation architects, we must take advantage of this desirable situation by creating, maintaining, facilitating and further improving the situations in our digital transformation programs.

Collaborative Influence

Our digital awareness and skills as architecting team can help influence our extended team members to collaborate more effectively. Influence is an essential strategic leadership attribute in digital transformation initiatives.

Influence is particularly essential to create a collaborative culture in modernising and transforming our legacy environments. As transformation architects and architecting team, our influence can make a substantial impact on moving towards transformed environments.

As digital transformation architects, we influence our collaborators by demonstrating responsibility, accountability, and credibility in our actions. Due to its importance for digital transformation, we need to discuss credibility in the next section.

Credibility

Credibility in dynamic environments such as digital transformation teams can be critical. In other words, as digital transformation architects responsible for transforming environments, we must be credible at all times.

Promoting change in our dynamic environment and obtaining buy-in for transforming from our stakeholders and team members require demonstrated credibility.

As transformation architects, we can earn the trust of our collaborators with credibility and integrity. Our vision, strategy, knowledge, skills, actions have an impact on our credibility. Our architecting goals and our organisations' business goals must align with these critical attributes.

We need to be mindful that consistency and predictability for our behaviour are critical factors for credibility in these dynamic environments. To survive, thrive, and succeed in our transformation goals, we must pay special attention to our behaviour to remain credible at all times in digitally transforming environments.

Trust and Collaborative Engagement

When we establish trust, another magic happens. People start sharing their true selves. They become more productive and more creative. A collaborative culture is an empowering contributor and enabler of modernising and transforming enterprises.

Digital transformation requires people from diverse background to engage in collaborative activities. Enabling diversity is a critical factor in creating collaborative teams and an inclusive culture.

Diversity is extra critical for modernisation and transformation goals due to the required creativity and innovation by people from different backgrounds, skills sets, and experiences.

One way of establishing diversity is demonstrating trust in our teams. It is important to highlight that only with trust and trusted environments, people can show their true identities. When people start showing their true self, a diverse culture starts flourishing. Diversity is an enhancer of collaboration and fusion required for successful digital transformation.

More importantly, with diversity, also innovation comes to the picture. We can notice it stronger and faster. Diverse ideas ignite and accelerate innovation. With this approach, we can create new options and choices. Connecting those choices and options also make a ripple effect on the culture. With this understanding, we can conclude that trust-based diversity can be a valuable contributor to modernisation and digital transformation programs.

Chapter Summary and Take Away Points

In its true meaning, collaboration refers to a team of people working together for mutual goals to achieve successful and synergetic outcomes.

Collaboration is essential to create synergy in digital transformation teams.

Fusion principles aim to bring individuals from various backgrounds, small groups with different purposes, various teams with differing capabilities, communities of practices with different missions under a single umbrella for serving a joint mission.

We don't wait for fusion to happen by itself. We know that nothing can happen by itself. Naturally, someone with leadership and architectural skills must initiate it.

Written communications can create some challenges, such as a careless piece of writing may cause some offence and kill the spirit of collaboration.

The magic of fusion starts with these repetitions. Successful repetitions make ripple effects for more success.

Diversity oriented magical aspect of fusion and collaboration leading to innovation is an ideal situation for transforming the enterprise.

Influence is particularly essential to create a collaborative culture in modernising and transforming our legacy environments.

Our vision, strategy, knowledge, skills, actions have an impact on our credibility. Our architecting goals and our organisations' business goals must align with these critical attributes.

Diverse ideas ignite and accelerate innovation. With this approach, we can create new options and choices. Connecting those choices and options also make a ripple effect on the culture.

Chapter 8: Leverage Emerging Technology & Tools

Purpose

In this section, we cover the prominent technologies and briefly introduce them by highlighting their importance for modernisation and digital transformation goals.

Instead of delving into details and providing an exhaustive list, our focus is only on foundational technologies which can make a real difference. Let's touch on the critical technologies and technical skills that transformation architects and the architecting team need to possess for leading successful modernisation and digital transformation initiatives.

Broad technology awareness is a mandatory attribute for digital transformation architects. We must be up-to-date with digital technologies and possess a wide range of vital technical knowledge and skills.

There are many growing and emerging technologies that we need to be conversant. As transformation architects, we must focus on using emerging technologies as enablers of the enterprise modernisation and digital transformation goals.

Enabling Technologies

The key technology enablers of enterprise modernisation and digital transformation goals are

Cloud Computing, Mobile technologies, IoT, Big Data, and AI-based or Cognitive Data Analytics.

An integrated view of these technologies, associated processes and tools are critical to our success in our digital endeavours. Besides, we must focus on benchmarking of technological products and services as they are essential enablers of our digital transformations. Let's start with Cloud Computing.

Cloud Computing

Nowadays, the most widely used technology in transforming enterprises is Cloud Computing. Cloud became mainstream in many organisations. Adoption of Cloud became very rapid. We can use Cloud as a foundational enterprise modernisation and digital transformation tool.

The most significant attribute of Cloud is that the cloud service model can expand or reduce computer resources based on service requirements. For example, Cloud can provide the maximum resources when we need a large amount of computing power, storage capacity, or network bandwidth for a specific workload at a particular timeframe. Then we can release these resources after completing our specific mission for these workloads. This elasticity and scalability of Cloud can provide value position for digital transformations.

'Pay per use' or 'pay as you go' is another essential characteristic that Cloud services model offers. The resources can be consumed based on the usage amount. Usage could be a short, medium, or long-term basis. For example, consumers can pay based on computing power or storage amount they used.

Related to 'pay per use', using 'on-demand' is another characteristic of the Cloud services model. Consumers can use when they demand the required services without upfront payment or dedicated investment for the IT resources in their organisation.

The recent commercial trend for using virtual machines in publicly available Cloud services are based on three types of instances such as on-demand instance, reserved instance, and spot instance.

In on-demand instance, there is no long-term commitment. Reserved instance is a relatively longer-term with a substantial discount compared to on-demand usage. For the spot instance, as commonly promoted by several service providers, the price is agreed based on bidding.

Cloud offers resiliency to the infrastructure, applications and services. System failures such as servers or storage units can be automatically isolated with predefined instructions, and our workloads are migrated to redundant virtual units without disrupting the service levels or consumer usage. Cloud's resilience attribute removes many of our supportability concerns in our solution requirements.

Based on consumer requirements, Cloud resources can be virtual or physical. This flexibility is created by multitenancy characteristic of the Cloud service model. For example, a Cloud service provider can host multiple user workloads in the same infrastructure without adversely affecting their privacy and security.

If there are high-security requirements such as sensitive governmental services, isolation can be physical. We need to consider constraints and limitations which can affect the use of virtual services in multi-tenancy mode.

Flexible workload movement is another crucial attribute of Cloud service model. There may be times an organisation requires to run their workloads in a different time zone, and the workloads can easily be moved to a data centre in another country.

Such requirements may be for several reasons such as reducing cost, providing a better service for a focus group in a different location or even regulatory requirements. Let's introduce the next important technology, IoT, which is proliferating.

IoT (Internet of Things)

After Cloud Computing, another rapidly emerging technology is the IoT (Internet of Things). As transformation architects, we need to understand this vital technology.

Substantial progress has been made in many disciplines owing to the use of IoT in creating new services and products. Some of these disciplines include environmental monitoring, manufacturing, infrastructure management, energy management, agriculture, healthcare, transportation, IT, electronics, material sciences and banking.

In the market, it is noticeable that IoT technologies are emerging and IoT solutions are growing exponentially to support digital transformation initiatives.

It is estimated that billions of devices in the next few years to connect to the global IoT ecosystem. The bottom line is that IoT is valuable for both business and economy, which is inevitable. From our current experience, we can construe that IoT can have a substantial impact on our economy and the way we do business and commerce as far as digital transformation are concerned.

Consumers and service providers have an incredible interest and focus on this fantastic technology powered by the internet. The generation of new business for companies and new job roles that we cannot even name yet is imminent.

Some believe that the IoT can be as important as the emergence of the internet itself. Some even point out that it can be the next big thing in our lives. These are, of course, speculations, combined with some media hype; however, time can tell as to whether the high expectations of IoT to be met.

As transformation architects and architecting team, we need to understand IoT offerings and possess a broad range of IoT knowledge and skills because IoT is one of the primary enablers of the modernisation and digital transformation initiatives to create new revenue streams and broader business opportunities. Our next critical technology domain is Big Data and AI-based Analytics.

Big Data and AI-Based Analytics

In addition to IoT, Big Data and AI-based Analytics are vital technologies and processes that we need to understand. Not only understand but also, we must use them for creating insights and competitive advantage for our digital transformation goals.

It is important to note that even though architecturally similar to traditional data, Big Data requires newer methods and tools to deal with data. The traditional methods and tools are not adequate to process big data especially for digital transformation goals.

The Big Data process refers to capturing a substantial amount of data from multiple sources, storing analysing, searching, transferring, sharing, updating, visualising and governing huge volumes data sets such as in petabytes or even exabytes nowadays.

Interestingly, the main concern or aim of Big Data is not the amount of data but more advanced AI-based or cognitive analytics techniques to produce value out of these large volumes of data. The advanced analytics in this context refers to approaches such as descriptive, predictive, prescriptive, and diagnostic analytics. These types of cognitive analytics types can be invaluable for our digital transformation initiatives.

We need to understand the type of analytics and when to use them for what type of transformation solutions. Each have different purpose and use cases for digital transformation goals. Let's explain briefly.

The descriptive analytics deals with situations such as what is happening right now based on incoming data. The predictive analytics refers to what might happen in the future. Prescriptive analytics deals with actions to be taken. Diagnostic analytics ask the question of why something happened. Each analytics type serves difference scenarios and use-cases.

AI-based Big Data Analytics is a comprehensive business-driven discipline. At a high level, it aims to make quick business decisions, reduce the cost for a product or service, and test new market to create new products and services.

All industries nowadays use AI-based Big Data analytics. For example, health care, life sciences, manufacturing, government, and retail are extensively using Big Data and Cognitive Analytics for new insights, creating business opportunities, and opening new markets.

We need new methods and tools to perform AI-based Big Data analytics. There are emerging methods and many tools available on the market. Most of the methods are proprietary, but some are available via open-source programs. For our awareness and consideration in our digital transformation initiatives, some popular tools frequently mentioned in the Big Data Analytics publications are Aqua Data Studio, Azure HDinsight, IBM SPSS Modeler, Skytree, Talend, Splice Machine, Plotly, Lumify, Elasticsearch.

Besides, open-source has progressed well in this area and produced multiple powerful tools. Some commonly used open-source analytics tools are from Apache organisation such as Hadoop, Spark, Storm, Cassandra, and SAMOA. The other frequently used open-source tools as Neo4j, MongoDB, and R programming environment. These tools are beyond our scope in this book, however it is useful to create awareness here as they are widely used in digital transformation initiatives.

Big Data analytics is a broad and growing area. We can better understand Big data analytics looking at its inherent characteristics. We can summarise these characteristics using terms such as connection, conversion, cognition, configuration, content, customisation, cloud, cyber, and community. These terms are associated with our day to day architectural practices and self-explanatory hence we don't go into details here.

We also need to familiarise ourselves with Big Data analytics methods and techniques that we can use in our digital transformation initiatives. Some of these methods and techniques are natural language processing, data mining, association pattern mining, behavioural analytics, predictive analytics, descriptive analytics, prescriptive analytics, diagnostic analytics, and machine learning.

Machine learning is a trending discipline for AI-based Big Data Analytics. It is widely adopted by many large organisations. The prime examples extensively using Machine Learning are Google and Amazon.

Machine learning refers to computer systems to learn and improve based on their learning from the analysis of large volumes of data sets without programming. It is part of the artificial intelligence domain in computer science. Due to its usefulness and impact, machine learning became a vital technology and tool for enterprise modernisation strategies leading to digital transformation. As transformation architects, we need to add machine learning to our digital transformation toolbox.

Related to machine learning, we also need to understand unstructured data handling, particularly text analytics. Text analytics leverage machine learning, computational linguistics, and traditional statistical analysis. Text analytics focus on converting massive volumes of a machine or human-generated text into meaningful structures to create business insights and support business decision-making.

There are various text analytics techniques that we need to familiarise. For example, information extraction is one of the text analytics techniques which extract structured data from unstructured text. This technique can be useful for some digital transformation initiatives.

Text summarisation is another widely used unstructured data processing technique which can automatically create a condensed summary of a document or selected groups of documents. We can use text summarization technique, especially for blogs, news, product documents, and scientific papers. There may be numerous use cases to apply text summarisation technique for digital transformation initiatives.

Natural Language Processing (NLP) is another sophisticated text analytics technique interfaced as question and answers in natural language. NLP is commonly used in various commercial products such as Siri by Apple, Watson by IBM, and Alexa by Amazon products. NLP can be an excellent enabler of some of our digital transformation goals and meet the requirements for providing natural language to our consumers.

Overall Security and Cybersecurity

In addition to analytics, security is the next critical knowledge and skill that we must possess as transformation architects. Particular security which we call cybersecurity is even more critical in digital transformation initiatives.

Cybersecurity touches every aspect of enterprise modernisation and digital transformation initiatives. Cybersecurity is a vast security domain covering every aspect of security management, such as identity and access management, authentication, authorisation, encryption, and many more crucial areas of security. Applying cybersecurity is a critical enabler for securing modernisation and digital transformation solutions.

The emerging technology stacks especially Cloud Computing, IoT, and Big Data also mandate cybersecurity at all levels. Broader security awareness and associated skills are essential for our digital transformation initiatives.

Related to advanced security, Blockchain, which is relatively new technology, is becoming critical for new security requirements which could be enablers for modernisation and digital transformation goals.

Blockchain

The Blockchain is based on decentralised technology framework. It is digital data management protocol with a network consists of nodes. It offers storage technology coupled with information transmission.

Blockchain allows all participants and transparent to everyone. The database of the Blockchain is distributed in nature. It keeps different copies simultaneously in different nodes.

The Blockchain protocol is based on peer-to-peer. In other words, it does not require a control body. More importantly it is believed to be infallible and secure. Unlike more conventional databases, it is "distributed". It means that different copies exist simultaneously on different computers of the network by preventing the Blockchain from being hacked. It is secure by design. The security framework for the Blockchain is supported by use of Byzantine fault tolerance.

The critical component of the Blockchain is the database. It has two kinds of records namely blocks and the transactions. Blocks hold batches of valid transactions. They are hashed and encoded into a Merkle tree. This is a term in cryptography. It is defined as a tree in which every non-leaf node is labelled with the cryptic hash of the labels or values of its child node.

The primary use case for Blockchain is identity management. This can allow us perform identity management in a decentralised manner. This powerful shift can allow us to own our data and to manage it as needed and others can trust us in the process. Blockchain is expected to evolve rapidly and transform into an inevitable and ubiquitous technology in less than a decade.

The Blockchain is still work in progress especially in the open-source communities. These communities continually update it. There is remarkably growing literature on the Blockchain in industry and academia. Several universities have already commenced conducting substantial research in developing and extending the Blockchain. Many large corporate organisations are creating awareness and make it part of their strategic path. It is time for us to consider applying the Blockchain to our digital transformation goals to meet new security requirements.

Network

As digital transformation architects, we deal with the network frequently. Enterprise modernisation and digital transformation solutions touch every aspect of networking such as wide area, local area, wireless and other networking types.

The network is a fundamental infrastructure component. Networks are enablers of Cloud, IoT, Blockchain, and Big Data analytics. It is so fundamental that these technology stacks cannot perform and even cannot exist without a network.

The network and associated communication technologies are the fundamental enablers of digital transformation goals. Understanding functions of network and network implications such as security, latency, bandwidth, are also important topics. These factors play an essential role in our digital transformation initiatives.

As transformation architects, we need to cover broadly and sometimes in-depth based on our involvement in various digital transformation initiatives. As we usually cover the breadth, it is beneficial to leverage skills of a network architect, technical specialists, network domain experts such as CCIEs (Cisco Certified Internetwork Experts), or other network subject matter experts to help us.

Mobility

Mobility is a critical interrelated technology domain in digitally transforming organisations moving to mobile solutions. As transformation architects, we need to understand and educate our architecting teams for the effective use of mobility for innovations leading to business insights and collaboration across the organisation including our customers and partners.

We also need to understand the domain of Enterprise Mobile Management. This domain includes essential components such as device management, application management, content management, email management, and unified endpoint management.

Mobility is associated with several architectural and business considerations such as network access, compliance, data management, workplace demographics, end-user accountability and BYOD (Bring Your Own Devices) practices in many organisations.

IT Service Management

IT service management is inevitable for transforming enterprises. IT service management covers an extensive array of technology, process, and tools. IT service management includes processes such as change management, problem management, incident management, service level management, capacity management, availability management, business continuity management, and security management.

In addition, system management processes such as monitoring, alerting and event management can be covered under the umbrella term of IT Service Management. These processes are managed using many technological tools. More importantly, these tools need to be architected, integrated, designed and implemented coherently for enterprise digital transformation goals.

Understanding the dynamics of these tools within the context of modernisation and digital transformation initiatives are vital for successful outcomes.

One of the best representations of IT Service model is implemented using popular ITIL (Information Technology Infrastructure Library. Knowledge of ITIL can be handy in communicating our service management needs to broader stakeholders in the digitally transforming enterprise.

Chapter Summary and Take Away Points

Broad technology awareness is a mandatory attribute for digital transformation architects.

The key technology enablers of enterprise modernisation and digital transformation goals are Cloud Computing, Mobile technologies, IoT, Big Data, and AI-based or Cognitive Data Analytics.

The most significant attribute of Cloud is that the cloud service model can expand or reduce computer resources based on service requirements.

'Pay per use' or 'pay as you go' is another essential characteristic that Cloud services model offers.

Flexible workload movement is another crucial attribute of Cloud service model. There may be times an organisation requires to run their workloads in a different time zone, and the workloads can easily be moved to a data centre in another country.

Some believe that the IoT can be as important as the emergence of the internet itself. Some even point out that it can be the next big thing in our lives.

Even though architecturally similar to traditional data, Big Data requires newer methods and tools to deal with data.

The Big Data process refers to capturing a substantial amount of data from multiple sources, storing analysing, searching, transferring, sharing, updating, visualising and governing huge volumes data sets such as in petabytes or even exabytes nowadays.

The descriptive analytics deals with situations such as what is happening right now based on incoming data. The predictive analytics refers to what might happen in the future. Prescriptive analytics deals with actions to be taken. Diagnostic analytics ask the question of why something happened. Each analytics type serves difference scenarios and use-cases.

AI-based Big Data Analytics is a comprehensive business-driven discipline. At a high level, it aims to make quick business decisions, reduce the cost for a product or service, and test new market to create new products and services.

We can better understand Big data analytics looking at its inherent characteristics such as connection, conversion, cognition, configuration, content, customisation, cloud, cyber, and community. These terms are associated with our day to day architectural practices and self-explanatory hence we don't go into details here.

Machine learning refers to computer systems to learn and improve based on their learning from the analysis of large volumes of data sets without programming. It is part of the artificial intelligence domain in computer science.

Text analytics leverage machine learning, computational linguistics, and traditional statistical analysis. Text analytics focus on converting massive volumes of a machine or human-generated text into meaningful structures to create business insights and support business decision-making.

Text summarisation is another widely used unstructured data processing technique which can automatically create a condensed summary of a document or selected groups of documents.

NLP is commonly used in various commercial products such as Siri by Apple, Watson by IBM, and Alexa by Amazon products.

Cybersecurity touches every aspect of enterprise modernisation and digital transformation initiatives.

The Blockchain is based on decentralised technology framework. It is digital data management protocol with a network consists of nodes. It offers storage technology coupled with information transmission.

The Blockchain protocol is based on peer-to-peer. In other words, it does not require a control body.

The primary use case for Blockchain is identity management.

Networks are enablers of Cloud, IoT, Blockchain, and Big Data analytics. It is so fundamental that these technology stacks cannot perform and even cannot exist without a network.

Mobility is a critical interrelated technology domain in digitally transforming organisations moving to mobile solutions.

We also need to understand the domain of Enterprise Mobile Management. This domain includes essential components such as device management, application management, content management, email management, and unified endpoint management.

One of the best representations of IT Service model is implemented using popular ITIL (Information Technology Infrastructure Library.

Chapter 9: Reconstruct Data

Purpose

Data is the most valuable asset in business intelligence. For good reasons, there is tremendous focus on data for digital transformations.

Applying data intelligence steers the transformation and leads to new business insights. One significant fact is that data, especially Big Data, is ubiquitous in every enterprise.

Large organisations generate massive amounts of data coming multiple sources. There are ongoing real-time data collection and analysis creating business value. The most prominent example is the data coming from embedded objects as we discussed in the IoT section.

As transformation architects and architecting team, data is our bread and butter for our digital transformation initiatives. Therefore, we need to understand every aspect of data in its lifecycle methodically. Let's start with Big Data.

Big Data for Digital Transformation

Big data is different from traditional data. The main differences come from characteristics such as volume, velocity, variety, veracity, value and overall complexity of data sets in a data platform or overall ecosystem.

Volume refers to the size or amount of data sets. We can measure them in terabytes, petabytes or exabytes. There are no specific definitions to determine the threshold for Big Data volumes. Ironically, even though it is called the Big Data, and it is a signifier, the volume is not the main characteristics of the Big Data as far as architecture, design and deployments are concerned.

Velocity refers to the speed of producing data. Big Data sources generate high-speed data streams coming from real-time devices such as mobile phones, social media, IoT sensors, IoT edge gateways, and the Cloud data stores. Velocity is an essential factor in all phases of the Big Data architecture and management considerations.

Variety refers to multiple sources of data. The data sources include structured transactional data, semi-structured such as web sites or system logs, and unstructured data such as video, audio, animation, and pictures. Variety is also a significant factor for Big Data architecture and management considerations.

Veracity means the quality of the data. Since volume and velocity are enormous in Big Data, veracity is very challenging. It is essential to have quality output to make sense of data for business insights. Veracity is also related to value.

Value is the primary purpose of Big Data to create new insights and gain business value from Big Data. We can create value with innovative and creative approaches taken by all the stakeholders of a Big Data solution.

Overall complexity for Big Data refers to more data attributes and difficulty to extract desired value due to large volume, wide variety, enormous velocity and required veracity for the desired value.

Even though architecturally similar to traditional data, Big Data requires newer methods and tools to deal with data. The traditional methods and tools are not adequate to process Big Data.

The Big Data process refers to capturing a substantial amount of data from multiple sources, storing analysing, searching, transferring, sharing, updating, visualising and governing huge volumes data in the magnitude of petabytes or even exabytes.

The main concern or aim of Big Data is not the amount of data but more advanced analytics techniques to produce value out of these large volumes of data. The advanced analytics in this context refers to approaches such as descriptive, predictive, prescriptive, and diagnostic analytics. Let's re-iterate the meaning of these techniques in a summary as they are crucial for digital transformations.

The descriptive analytics deals with situations such as what is happening right now based on incoming data. The predictive analytics refers to what might happen in the future. Prescriptive analytics deals with actions to be taken. Diagnostic analytics ask the question of why something happened. Each analytics type serves difference scenarios and use-cases. Now, let's move on to the data management lifecycle.

Data Management Lifecycle

For modernisation and digital transformation initiatives, we need to consider Big Data as a critical player in the enterprise and its ecosystem. Therefore, as transformation architects, we need to understand the lifecycle of Big Data for digital transformation goals.

Our roles and responsibilities may differ in different stages in the lifecycle; however, we need to be on top of the life cycle management, especially from the governance perspective, end to end in the digital transformation initiatives.

A typical Big Data solution, similar to traditional data lifecycle, includes several distinct phases in the overall data lifecycle management. We participate in all phases of the lifecycle, providing different input for each stage.

These phases may have different names in different data solution teams. Enterprise Architects or Transformation architects, depending to the structure of the transformation program, create a standard naming convention for the phases to bring everyone on the same page.

Let's keep in mind that there is no rigorous universal systematic approach to the Big Data lifecycle as the discipline is still evolving. Names and approaches are continually changing based on ongoing experimentations.

At a high level, the data management lifecycle can include foundations, acquisitions, preparation, input, processing, output, interpretation, analytics, consumptions, retention, backup, recovery, archival, and destruction.

As transformation architects, we get involved in all these stages; hence, a broad knowledge of these phases can be beneficial to gain data management awareness. Let's briefly touch on the phases.

Foundation phase includes understanding and validating data requirements, solution scope, roles and responsibilities of stakeholders, data infrastructure preparation, technical and non-technical considerations, and understanding data rules in an organisation.

The foundation phase requires a detailed plan facilitated ideally by a project manager with substantial input from the Big Data solution architects. A PDR (project definition report) must cover the non-technical matters such as project funding, commercials, and other issues. Enterprise architects govern this phase at enterprise level and transformation architects cover it within transformation program scope.

Data Acquisition phase refers to collecting data. We can obtain data from various sources. These sources can be internal and external to the organisation.

Data sources can be structured forms such as transferred from a data warehouse, transaction systems, or semi-structured forms such as Web or system logs, or unstructured such as media files consist of videos, audios or pictures.

Data governance, security, privacy, and quality controls start with the data collection phase. The lead data architects document the data collection strategy, requirements, architectural decisions, use cases, and technical specifications in this phase. Transformation architects may need to review and approve the requirements and architectural decisions affecting the digital transformation initiatives. Data and platform specialists review and approve the specifications.

In the data preparation phase, we clean the collected raw data. We check the data rigorously for any inconsistencies, errors, and duplicates. We consistently remove any redundant, duplicated, incomplete and incorrect data sets and entries. This activity results in having a clean data set. Preparation of data is usually a specialist level task; however, transformation architects may need to govern this phase. They can delegate specific activities to the data solution architects and specialists.

Data input refers to sending data to planned target data repositories or systems. For example, we send the clean data to determined destinations such as CRM systems, data lakes, or data warehouse. In this phase, we transform the raw data into a useable format. Usually, an Enterprise Architect governs this phase;

however, transformation architects may get involved in architecture board activities.

Data Processing starts with processing the raw form of data. Then, we convert data into a readable format giving it the form and context. After this activity, we can interpret data by the selected data analytics tools. We can use generic or proprietary Big Data processing tools based on the data practices in our organisation.

Some standard tools that we may consider are Hadoop MapReduce, Impala, Hive, Pig, and Spark SQL. The most commonly used real-time data processing tool is HBase, and near real-time data processing tools is Spark Streaming. Data processing also includes activities such as data annotation, integration, aggregation, and representation.

In this phase, data may change its format based on requirements. We can use processed data in various data outputs such as in data lakes, for enterprise networks, and connected devices. We can further analyse data using advanced processing techniques and tools such as Spark MLib, Spark GraphX, and machine learning.

Data processing require various team members with different skills sets. While the lead solution architect leads the phase, data specialists, engineers and data scientists perform most of the activities. Enterprise Architects govern this phase from approach, process, technology and tool perspective.

Transformation architects participate in governance activities for the digital transformation programs.

Data output is a phase where the data is in a format ready for consumption by the business users. We can transform data into useable formats such as plain text, graphs, processed images or video files. This phase announces the data ready for use and sends the data to the next stage for storing.

Data output phase in some organisation is also called data ingestion aiming to export data for immediate use or future use and keep it in a database format. Ingestion process can be a real-time or batch format. We must familiarise with standard Big Data ingestion tools such as Sqoop, Flume, and Spark streaming.

Once we complete the data output phase, we store data in allocated storage units as pointed out by the data platform designs. Once data is stored, then it can be easily accessed by the defined user groups. Big Data storage includes underlying technologies such as relational data storage or extended data storage such as HDFS and HBASE.

We can consider the file formats text, binary, or another type of specialised formats such as Sequence, Avro, and Parquet in data storage phase. Several architects and specialists participate in this phase. While transformation architects work with the Enterprise Architects to set the standards, Infrastructure Architects build the data platforms with the input from the Data or Information Architects.

Once the data is stored, in traditional models, it ends the process. However, for Big Data, there may be a need for the integration of stored data for various purposes. Some data models may require integration of data lakes with a data warehouse or data marts.

There may also be application integration requirements. For example, some integration activities may comprise of integrating data with dashboards, tableau, websites, or data visualisations applications. This activity may overlap with the next phase, which is data analytics.

Integrated data is ready for data analytics, which is the next phase. Data analytics is a significant component of Big Data. This phase is critical because we gain business value from Big Data. There can be a team responsible for data analytics led by a Data Scientist. Data Architect has a limited role in this phase. Data Architects need to ensure we complete this phase using architectural rigour for analytics. Enterprise Architects validate the standards. Transformation architects can provide guidance and requirements clarification of analytics within their scope.

Once data analytics takes place, then we turn data into information ready for consumption by the internal or external users, including customers of the organisation. Some critical data may need to be backed up. There are data backup strategies, techniques, methods and tools that the digital leaders may need to provide guidance to identify, document, and obtain approval.

We may need to archive some critical data for regulatory or other business reasons for a defined period. With the input from digital leaders, Enterprise or Transformation Architects determine, and document data retention strategy approved by the governing body in the data practice department.

There may be regulatory requirements to destruct a particular type of data after a certain amount of times. These may change based on the industries that data belong. Even though there is a chronological order for the life cycle management, for producing Big Data solutions, some phases may slightly overlap; hence, we can perform them in parallel.

The life cycle is a guideline and can be customised based on the structure of the data solution team, data needs and dynamics of the owner organisation's departments or the enterprise.

Usually, Data Architects begins with an understanding of the process end to end. We can classify the process under two broad categories. The first one is Data Management, and the second one is Data Analytics.

It can be useful to understand data management activities such as data acquisition, extraction, cleansing, annotation, processing, integration, aggregation, and representation. Data Analytics components at a high level are activities such as modelling, analysis, interpretation, and visualisation.

Data Platforms

We need to understand the function of data platforms in our digital transformation initiatives. The first layer of the data platform is the shared operational information zone consists of the data types such as data in motion, data at rest, and data in several other forms.

This first layer includes legacy data sources, new data sources, master data hubs, reference data hubs, and content repositories.

The second large layer is processing. This layer includes data ingestion, operational information, landing area, analytics zone, archive, real-time analytics, exploration, integrated warehouse, data mart zones.

The second layer needs to have a governance model for metadata catalogue including data security and disaster recovery of systems, storage and hosting and other infrastructure components such as Cloud.

The third layer is the analytics platform. It consists of real-time analytics, planning, forecasting, decision making, predictive analytics, data discovery, visualisations, dashboard, and other analytics features.

The fourth layer consists of outputs such as business processes, decision-making schemes, and point of interactions. We need to provide access with established controls both for the data platform professionals such as Data Scientists, Data Architects, analytics experts, and business users. We need to engage a Security Architect or Specialist to analyse the requirements and take appropriate measures.

Level of the schema for the data platform is a crucial architectural consideration. We can classify the level of schema under three categories, such as no schema, partially structured schema, and full structured schema. Control of schema is an enterprise concern; therefore, Enterprise Architects need to take control of this function with input from transformation architects.

To understand the type of schema, we can use examples. Some examples of no schema are video, audio and picture files; social media feed, partial schema such as email, instant messaging logs, system logs, call centre logs; and high schema can be structured sensor data and relational transaction data.

The data processing levels require architectural considerations. The processing levels could be raw data, validated data, transformed data and calculated data. Another structural classification of data in this platform is related the business relevance. We can categorise the business relevance of data as external data, personal data, departmental data and enterprise data.

Business Vocabulary

Another essential concept in data management is business vocabulary. We need to define business vocabulary as a shared understanding of Big Data related to business analytics.

Business vocabulary provides consistent terms to be used by the whole organisation. Business departments own business vocabulary. Enterprise Architects ensure that this is in place and adequately governed.

Usually, business users maintain this vocabulary. This vocabulary describes the business content supported by the data models. More importantly, from an architectural perspective, this vocabulary can be a crucial input to the metadata catalogue; hence, it can be an enterprise concern or transformation program concern.

Data Governance in Digital Transformation

We must govern data in our transformation programs. Data governance is a critical factor for digital transformation.

For the Big Data governance, we need to consider essential factors such as security, privacy, trust, operability, conformance, agility, innovation and transformation of data.

It is also vital that at a fundamental level, a data governance infrastructure to be established and evolve for adoption at the transformation program or enterprise level in an integrated manner.

Governance may take consideration for different stakeholders in the enterprise and its data ecosystem. For example, Data Architects are responsible for developing the governance of Big Data models. Data Scientist is accountable for an analytics perspective. Business stakeholders are responsible for the governance of business models for producing business results for the data ecosystem in concern.

Big Data governance is a broad area and covers components, scope, requirements handling, strategy, architecture, design, development, analysis, tests, processing, components, relationships, input, output, business goals, insights, and all other aspects of data management and analytics.

As transformation architects, we must closely work with Enterprise Architects to maintain governance, especially for digital transformation programs.

Enterprise Architects are responsible for end to end governance of Big Data architecture and the associated solutions at the enterprise level. They may delegate some governance tasks with Big Data lead and solution architects as required. As transformation architects, our focus is always on the digitally transforming environments within our scope.

Data Lakes

Big Data digital transformation solutions require the use of the data lake model. Data lakes are fundamental and useful aspects of Big Data lifecycle management. Let's define and explain it.

We can define data lakes in the simplest terms as the dynamically clean and instantly useable data sources made available for specific purposes.

The need for data lakes come from users to take advantage of clean data based on self-service approach without needing technical data professionals. Use of data lakes can be a critical business proposition for enterprise modernisation and digital transformation programs.

A data lake can be a single store of transformed enterprise data in the native format. They are usually well reported, visualised and analysed using advanced analytics. A data lake can include structured, semi-structured, and unstructured data such as images, videos, or sounds.

Data lakes are dynamic stores and can be fed iteratively as further clean data are discovered and transformed from multiple sources in the enterprise. For example, a data lake can store relational data from enterprise applications and non-relational data from IoT devices, social media, and mobile apps.

There are multiple use cases for data lakes. The most common ones are when real-time data analysis required for the data sources coming from various sources. Another use case can be related to the goals of having a complete view of customer data again coming from multiple sources. Auditing requirements and centralisation of data can also be use cases for data lakes. These use cases are relevant and can be significant for enterprise modernisation goals.

The business value of data lakes come from being able to perform advanced analytics very quickly for data coming from various real-time sources such as clickstreams, social media, system logs. Use of data lakes helps the business stakeholders to identify opportunities rapidly, make informed decisions, and act on their decision expeditiously for speed to the market.

Data lakes can be implemented using various tools, techniques, and services. There are commercially available services as well as open-source services to establish data lakes. For example, commercial products such as Azure Data Lake, Amazon S3 and open source product Apache Hadoop file system are some data lake implementation enablers to consider for our solutions. There are many more tools and methods to design, implement and execute data lake solutions.

Based on feedback obtained from many successful implementations of data lakes, it appears that an excellent choice of platform for data lakes is Hadoop. Hadoop, as an open-source system, is highly scalable, modular, technology agnostic, cost-effective and presents no schema limitations. I observed that many digital transformation architects I worked with and met in other organisations embraced Hadoop due to its effectiveness for transformations.

Designing data lakes require critical consideration of data types. For example, one key consideration is that if the purpose of data is unknown, it is better to keep data in raw format so that it can be used by data professionals in the future when it is needed. Transformation architects can guide these decisions at the program level as far as digital transformations are concerned.

One of the critical challenges of data lakes is security as the data comes to the lake in real-time from multiple uncontrolled sources. To address this challenge, a well-governing security architecture with access controls and semantic consistency need to be in place for the enterprise data lake.

Data lake design is a specialist level activity usually conducted by an experienced storage architect or specialist. Transformation architects may provide input to set the standards and maintain the governance for the lifecycle of data lake initiatives.

In addition to data lakes, we also need to understand the data puddles and ponds. Data puddle is a tiny purpose-build data platform usually used by a specific single team mission in an organisation conducted by a marketing group or data scientist. They are also a right candidate for data-intensive ETL (Extract, Transform, Load) offloading engagements for a single team. Unlike data lakes, they are not data-driven processing allowing informed decisions at enterprise levels.

Related to data puddles, another term used for a group of data puddles is data ponds. We can design data ponds for a small amount of data management purposes. One way of explaining a data pond is to resemble it to a data warehouse designed for Big Data processing.

Transformation architects can provide necessary input for choosing the right data deployment model with the help of Enterprise, Data and Information Architects.

One more essential term related to data lakes that we need to understand is 'data swamp'. This term refers to an unmanaged data lake that may not be accessible by the intended consumers or may not provide desired business value. From lessons learned in the field, many unsuccessful implementations of data lakes, unfortunately, turned into data swamps.

Let's keep in mind that data swamps are undesirable situations in an enterprise and digital transformation initiatives. Thus, as transformation architects, we need to consider these types of hard-learned lessons for data management strategy of the enterprise modernisation and digital transformation plans.

Essential Considerations for Data Solutions

As transformation architects, we leverage architectural skills, relevant technology, and tools to create custom solutions for digital transformations. The custom solutions can be products or services depending on the goals and the scope of the digital transformation programs.

Big Data solutions are distinct and require additional expertise. In addition to considering several architectural points, these solutions also require domain knowledge of data and information architecture.

At the highest level, we need to identify optimal approaches to collecting, storing, processing, analysing, and presenting Big Data. However, practical solutions are architected by Big Data or Information Architects with our guiding input.

Big Data solutions require heterogeneous technology and tools to fit the purpose. It is essential to realise that there is no single technology or tool which can provide all-purpose for developing Big Data solutions.

Besides, due to their dependencies and relationships to many components, attributes, and factors, Big Data solutions cannot be developed in isolation or silos. Transformation architects need to consider the entire ecosystem and break the silos in thinking and critical architectural factors that may affect the whole enterprise.

For Big Data solutions, we must focus on highly-scalable platforms, processes, technology, and tools. Due to its nature, scalability is a fundamental requirement for Big Data solutions. Compromising scalability, even in a small amount, can cause undesirable solutions, troubled projects, and failed service levels. Scalability is a critical factor for enterprise modernisation and digital transformation initiatives.

Modularity is another essential consideration for Big Data solutions for digital transformation goals. For modularity, we need to ensure the modules fits into the big picture. For example, the same data should be able to be used by different projects in a program and technology stacks rather than creating unnecessary data access silos.

Big Data solutions for digital transformation requires thinking out of the box and innovative ways of doing things. We need to understand the latest technologies and practices for Big Data solutions. For example, there is a trend in the industry for trying new methods of data analysis without binding to traditional EDW resources and ETL processes.

In terms of tools and technologies, we can consider mixing open source and commercial systems based on their applicability and meeting our requirements. For example, OLTP can be designed using commercially available relational databases for structured and open-source Casandra Database supporting semi-structured databases.

Data sources in the enterprise keep changing, and new sources are being available. In addition to legacy data sources, we need to consider new data sources in Big Data modernisation and digital transformation solutions. We need to determine the type of data sources required in our solutions.

From solution readiness and quality management perspectives, it is vital to determine the timelines of data ingestion in the enterprise. Data ingestion, as a critical aspect of Big Data in the modernisation context, is the process of importing, transferring, loading processing and storing data for use.

Data can be transferred as synchronous, or an asynchronous batched, or rea-time basis. We need to articulate these options with compelling reasons and obtain validating input and approvals from subject matter experts and the solution governance body.

It is vital to choose the type of processing to perform whether real-time or batch processing. Our data processing may involve descriptive, predictive, prescriptive, diagnostic, an ad-hoc. We also need to consider the latency expectation of processing. These factors can plan an important role in enterprise modernisation initiatives.

We need to determine how to access the data, for example, by random or sequential order. Besides, we need to consider data access patterns. Data access patterns are necessary to optimise data access requirements. There are many patterns available in data application integration and interface publications. For example, some common patterns are accelerating database resource initialisation, eliminating data access bottlenecks, and hiding obscure database semantics from data users.

Database optimisation is an essential practice at the enterprise level. These techniques aim to improve the quality and speed for data access, read and write activities. Some of the critical considerations are using appropriate indexes, removing unnecessary indexes and minimising data transfers from client to server.

So far, we provided a very high-level view of data considerations at the enterprise level. These are the only tip of the iceberg in developing Big Data solutions for digital transformation.

Transformation architects don't go into the details of Big Data design and deployment as it is specialist-level expertise rather than program or enterprise-level concern.

Once we start the process and delve into requirements, we can come across many more considerations based on our industry, project goals and many other factors which some of them can be beyond our controls and may require domain expertise.

Therefore, it is essential to follow an established data management method, collaborative solution team, proven processes, leading technology stacks, and well-supported tools to produce successful Big Data solutions for digital transformations.

As transformation architects, we can guide the team with these critical foundational data practices and always stay on top of the program level data requirements for our digital transformation initiatives.

As we use a lot of open-source data platform products and tools, it can be beneficial to further understand the importance of open-source for our digital transformation programs.

Open Source Data Platforms

I want to highlight the importance of using open-source tools for digital transformations, especially in the data platforms. Use of open source tools can be very beneficial for enterprise modernisation and digital transformation programs.

We all are aware of open source but in the case due to its importance let's briefly touch on the commonly used and recommended Big Data tools in the open-source space.

Open source is incredibly useful and widespread for information technology hence equally crucial for data analytics in the enterprise. It is a type licensing agreement which allows the developers and users to freely use the software, modify it, develop new ways to improve it and integrate to larger projects. It is a collaborative and innovative approach embraced by many IT organisations and consumer organisations. It is not only ideal for start-up companies and those companies with a tight IT budget but also enterprises struggling to have more flexible architectures for modernisation leading to digital transformations.

There are many open-source tools and technologies for Big Data and Analytics. Being familiar with some essential and commonly used open-source tools can be useful. An awareness of these tools is fundamental for us.

Here's a summary of the famous open-source Big Data and Analytics tools. Let's start with famous Hadoop. Apache Hadoop is a platform for data storage and processing. Hadoop is scalable, fault-tolerant, flexible, cost-effective and open source. It is ideal for handling massive storage pools using the batch approach in distributed computing environments. We can use Hadoop for complex Big Data and Analytics solutions at the enterprise level.

The next is Cassandra. Apache Cassandra is a semi-structured open source database. It is linearly scalable, high speed, and fault-tolerant. The primary use case for Cassandra is a transactional system requiring fast response and massive scalability. Cassandra is also widely used for Big Data and Analytics solutions at the enterprise level.

Apache Kafka is a stream processing software platform. Using Kafka, users can subscribe to commit logs and publish data to any number of systems or real-time applications. Kafka offers a unified, high-throughput, low-latency platform for real-time handling data feeds. Kafka platforms were initially developed by LinkedIn, used for a while, and donated to open source.

Apache Flume offers a simple and flexible architecture. The architecture of Flume is a reliable, distributed software for efficiently collecting, aggregating, and moving large amounts of log data in the Big Data ecosystem. We can use Flume for streaming data flows. Flume is fault-tolerant with many failover and recovery systems. Flume uses an extensible data model that allows for online analytic application.

Apache NiFi is an automation tool designed to automate the flow of data amongst the software components based on flow-based programming model. Currently, Cloudera supports for its commercial and development requirements. It has a portal for the users and uses TLS encryption for security.

Apache Samza is a near-real-time stream processing system. It provides an asynchronous framework for stream processing. Samza allows building stateful applications that process data in real-time from multiple sources. It is well known for offering fault tolerance, stateful processing, and isolation.

Apache Sqoop is a command-line interface application used to transfer data between Apache Hadoop and the relational databases. We can use it for incremental loads of a single table or free form SQL queries. We can use Sqoop with Hive and HBase to populate the tables.

Apache Chukwa is a system for data collection. Chukwa monitors large distributed systems and builds on the MapReduce framework on HDFS (Hadoop Distributed File System). Chukwa is a scalable, flexible and robust system for data collection.

Apache Storm is a stream processing framework. The Storm is based on spouts and bolts to define data sources. It allows batch and distributed processing of streaming data. The Storm also enables real-time data processing.

Apache Spark is a framework that allows cluster computing for distributed environments. We can use Spark for general clustering needs. It provides fault tolerance and data parallelism. Spark's architectural foundation is based on the resilient distributed dataset. The Dataframe API is an abstraction on top of the resilient distributed dataset. Spark has different editions, such as Core, SQL, Streaming, and GraphX.

Apache Hive is a data warehouse software. We can build Hive on Hadoop platform. Hive provides data query and supports the analysis of large datasets stored in HDFS. It offers a query language called HiveQL.

Apache HBase is a non-relational distributed database. HBase runs on top of HDFS. HBase provides Google's Bigtable-like capabilities for Hadoop. HBase is a fault-tolerant system.

Another great tool, non-Apache is MongoDB. It is a high performance, fault-tolerant, scalable, cross-platform and NoSQL database. It deals with unstructured data. It is developed by MongoDB Inc is licensed under the SSPL (Server-Side Public License), which is a kind of open-source product.

There are many more rapidly developing open-source software tools which can be used for various functions of data life cycle management in the enterprise. These tools can be handy for enterprise modernisation and transformation programs focusing on Big Data and Analytics solutions. These tools are easily accessible and available based on open source licencing agreements.

Commercial Tools

There are also many commercially available tools and technologies for Big Data and Analytics suitable to deploy across enterprise-wide solutions. These tools and technologies can be sold as products or services.

As transformation architects, we need to be aware of these products and services as they can be beneficial for our digital transformation initiatives.

Some of the most popular Big Data and Analytics platforms with associated tools are Google BigQuery, Hortonworks Data Platform, HP Bigdata, IBM Big Data, Microsoft Azure, SAP Bigdata Analytics, Teradata Bigdata Analytics, Amazon Web Services.

As coverage of these platforms and tools is comprehensive and exhaustive, it is beyond the scope of this book to include them here. I highly recommend reading the white papers of these products before imitating your architectural activities and especially before making any architectural decisions.

Chapter Summary and Take Away Points

Applying data intelligence steers the transformation and leads to new business insights. One significant fact is that data, especially Big Data, is ubiquitous in every enterprise.

Big data is different from traditional data. The main differences come from characteristics such as volume, velocity, variety, veracity, value and overall complexity of data sets in a data platform or overall ecosystem.

The Big Data process refers to capturing a substantial amount of data from multiple sources, storing analysing, searching, transferring, sharing, updating, visualising and governing huge volumes data in the magnitude of petabytes or even exabytes.

At a high level, the data management lifecycle can include foundations, acquisitions, preparation, input, processing, output, interpretation, analytics, consumptions, retention, backup, recovery, archival, and destruction.

This first layer includes legacy data sources, new data sources, master data hubs, reference data hubs, and content repositories.

The second layer includes data ingestion, operational information, landing area, analytics zone, archive, real-time analytics, exploration, integrated warehouse, data mart zones.

The third layer is the analytics platform. It consists of real-time analytics, planning, forecasting, decision making, predictive analytics, data discovery, visualisations, dashboard, and other analytics features.

The fourth layer consists of outputs such as business processes, decision-making schemes, and point of interactions.

Business vocabulary provides consistent terms to be used by the whole organisation. Business departments own business vocabulary.

For the Big Data governance, we need to consider essential factors such as security, privacy, trust, operability, conformance, agility, innovation and transformation of data.

Big Data governance is a broad area and covers components, scope, requirements handling, strategy, architecture, design, development, analysis, tests, processing, components, relationships, input, output, business goals, insights, and all other aspects of data management and analytics.

We can define data lakes in the simplest terms as the dynamically clean and instantly useable data sources made available for specific purposes.

Data lakes are dynamic stores and can be fed iteratively as further clean data are discovered and transformed from multiple sources in the enterprise. Designing data lakes require critical consideration of data types.

Big Data solutions are distinct and require additional expertise. In addition to considering several architectural points, these solutions also require domain knowledge of data and information architecture.

Modularity is another essential consideration for Big Data solutions for digital transformation goals.

In addition to legacy data sources, we need to consider new data sources in Big Data modernisation and digital transformation solutions.

Open source is incredibly useful and widespread for information technology hence equally crucial for data analytics in the enterprise. It is a type licensing agreement which allows the developers and users to freely use the software, modify it, develop new ways to improve it and integrate to larger projects.

Some of the most popular Big Data and Analytics platforms with associated tools are Google BigQuery, Hortonworks Data Platform, HP Bigdata, IBM Big Data, Microsoft Azure, SAP Bigdata Analytics, Teradata Bigdata Analytics, Amazon Web Services.

Chapter 10: Mobilise Building Blocks

Purpose

We use and work with mobile devices every day. Mobile Intelligence is critical to enterprise modernisation and digital transformation goals. Mobility is so crucial that the whole digital approach revolves around enterprise, product and services mobility. We need to architect mobility with the utmost care and rigorous methodical approach.

Importance of Mobility

Mobility involves people, process, technology and tools at a massive scale in every organisation. Mobility is essential for people and their work engagements in the enterprise.

The demand for mobility is rapidly increasing in all walks of life. The process for mobility is also challenged to meet the demands of consumers. In one way or another everyone in our society are affected by mobile technology and processes.

Mobile technology and tools are proliferating on the market. Mobile devices, mobile phones, mobile computers, tablets, wireless networks are a few to mention. It is not feasible to have a digital transformation initiative without extensively using mobile technology stacks.

Mobility Lifecycle Management

Lifecycle management for mobile devices is an essential architectural consideration in enterprise modernisation and digital transformation initiatives.

Managing mobile devices can be daunting from many angles. The life cycle for mobile devices can be much shorter than traditional computing and telecommunication devices.

One of the primary challenges related to the lifecycle of mobile devices is dealing with quantity. In the past, there were only office phones and people used to share them. Nowadays, workers have multiple mobile phones. Having multiple mobile devices per person may equate to thousands of mobile devices to consider at the enterprise level.

In addition to quantity, the user in the enterprise may change the mobile devices frequently. These frequent changes require consideration of applications and software updates for these devices in the dynamic lifecycle.

Enterprise modernisation and digital transformation strategies must consider the challenges associated with the lifecycle of these mobile devices. As transformation architects, we need to create dynamic and flexible governance to address the concerns related to the use and lifecycle management of these devices in our digital transformation initiatives.

Mobile Security Implications

The security implications of mobile devices are massive challenges. They create many security vulnerabilities for enterprises. Software updates can be persistent and very frequent. Frequent updates and patching can create a massive workload for the IT support departments. These challenges inevitably affect our digital transformation programs.

Use of these mobile devices increases information consumption in the enterprise dramatically. Security control of the data can be daunting too. These security implications cross the data and application domains; hence, a collaborative effort among the Security, Data and Application Architects are required. As transformation architects, we must coordinate this collaboration across other technical, architectural and business domains in our programs.

These critical challenges created by mobile devices are real and evident in the enterprise. Therefore, enterprise modernisation initiatives and digital transformation programs must consider these challenges and find practical and innovative ways to address them. We touched the importance of cybersecurity in previous chapters.

Mobile Business Intelligence

Mobile business intelligence, also known as Mobile BI is an essential requirement for enterprises to stay competitive, open new markets, and create new revenue streams. Mobile BI includes both real-time and historical information for analysing mobile devices such as phones and tablets. The primary purpose of Mobile BI is to provide insights, based on past and current information, for business decision making.

Mobile BI is necessary for the overall support of mobile devices in the enterprise ecosystem. This intelligence, providing a broad perspective on the business data, sales figures, consumption figures and performance statistics, can be valuable for enterprise modernisation.

Using the analytics on mobile progress in enterprise digital transformation initiatives can be instrumental to develop new business models and improve the current models.

Product and service providers widely use Mobile BI. Some established and popular Mobile BI environments are publicly accessible services such as Appstore by Apple, Google Play Store, and Samsung Galaxy Store.

Our digital transformation programs can model these well-functioning services to create and improve our current Mobile BI strategy, service models, and offerings.

Unified Endpoint Management

A unified endpoint management (UEM) practice is essential for enterprise modernisation and digital transformation initiatives. UEM includes relevant software tools and centralised management interfaces for consumers.

This centralisation is necessary to improve the security capabilities and also allow a collaborative content sharing for the consumers and other stakeholders. We need to integrate unified endpoint management to our enterprise modernisation program structure.

Conclusive Remarks for Mobility

Mobility is an inevitable part of our lives at home and in the workplace. Fortunately, or unfortunately, it created a bridge between homes and workplaces. In some ways, employers can easily access their employees; however, the privacy of employees are affected by this easy accessibility.

The reality is that we cannot do business without the use of mobile devices any more. Mobility is an essential part of the enterprise and all digital transformation programs. It touches every aspect of the workplace. We cannot have a digital workplace without proper mobility architecture in place.

We cannot transform our legacy enterprise without including the mobility to the equation. Due to these compelling reasons, we must approach mobility from strategic and architectural perspectives to properly integrate it into the culture and ecosystem of the modernising and digital transformation of our organisations.

Chapter Summary and Take Away Points

Mobility involves people, process, technology and tools at a massive scale in every organisation. Mobility is essential for people and their work engagements in the enterprise.

Lifecycle management for mobile devices is an essential architectural consideration in enterprise modernisation and digital transformation initiatives.

One of the primary challenges related to the lifecycle of mobile devices is dealing with quantity.

Security control of the data can be daunting too. These security implications cross the data and application domains; hence, a collaborative effort among the Security, Data and Application Architects are required.

Product and service providers widely use Mobile BI. Some established and popular Mobile BI environments are publicly accessible services such as Appstore by Apple, Google Play Store, and Samsung Galaxy Store.

A unified endpoint management (UEM) practice is essential for enterprise modernisation and digital transformation initiatives. UEM includes relevant software tools and centralised management interfaces for consumers.

We cannot transform our legacy enterprise without including the mobility to the equation.

Chapter 11: Create Smart Objects

Purpose

Our purpose in this chapter is to discuss the importance of smart objects combined with the power of the Internet. Yes, as you may guess, we are talking about the Internet of Things (IoT). IoT is one of the major pillars in our digital transformation method. As IoT is ubiquitous, it is an inevitable factor for the success of our digital transformation goals.

IoT Value Propositions

The main benefit and value proposition of IoT comes from collecting an enormous amount of data from various means and devices in the enterprise and then building services based on analyses of these massive amounts of data. Developing new services from such a collection of data would result in a substantial outcome with multiple architectural and business implications.

Business embrace IoT because it helps us predict the future; hence, the more data provided by the IoT systems, the better the analyses and outcomes can be. These data-rich analyses help us predict the future better and intervene before any potential damage occurs.

As we are able to synthesise IoT data via cognitive analytics, IoT solutions can help us gain better insights from structured, semi-structured, unstructured, dynamic or static data by integrating with cognitive systems.

Like humans, a cognitive system undertakes the duties of learning, understanding, planning, problem-solving, deciding, analysing, synthesising and assessing.

We can use IoT solutions in many facets of the enterprise. These solutions can be used for transformation of department, enterprise-wide, and external entities to the enterprise to predict what we need and want.

For digital transformation purposes, as an extended electronic ecosystem, IoT solutions can help to eliminate cumbersome technology affecting the performance of our organisations.

IoT can offer several applications at large scale for enterprises serving different industries. Some typical applications of IoT solutions are industrial control, robotics, medical, workplace safety, and security, embedded sensing in buildings, remote control, traffic control and most recently self-driving cars.

Architectural Implications of IoT Data

From an architectural perspective, we need to be aware that IoT devices generate massive amounts of data on an ongoing basis. These data sets go to the full data management life cycle; for example, in storing, analysing, re-building, and archiving.

Considering the scalability requirements for digital transformations, we must carefully consider the amount of data produced by IoT devices. The voluminous data in the enterprise require careful performance, scalability, usability, security, and availability measures.

When dealing with IoT in the digital transformation programs, as transformation architects, we must take the responsibility of data management requirements at the program level. We need to simulate the actual workload models based on the functional and non-functional requirements. We also need to consider historical data and future growth as part of the requirements analysis for performance.

Due to potential implications for enterprise and our transformation programs, we must plan data collection via IoT sensors carefully. First, we need to determine the type of physical signals to measure.

Then, we need to identify the number of sensors to be used and the speed of signals for these sensors in our data acquisition plan. Transformation architects need to closely work with the IoT Solution Architects to create stringent governance around data collection plans.

In addition to the challenges of massive data, application usage patterns are also an essential factor for the performance of IoT solutions in the enterprise modernisation and digital transformation initiatives. In particular, the processors and memory of the servers hosting the IoT applications need to be considered carefully using benchmarks.

Using benchmarks for application, data, and infrastructure, we need to create an exclusive IoT performance model and a set of test strategies for our transformation solutions.

The IoT performance model mandates more data storage capacity, faster processes, more memory, and faster network infrastructure. While in the traditional performance models, we mainly consider user simulations, in the IoT Performance models, we also consider the simulation of devices, sensors, and actuators across the enterprise.

From a data management perspective, it is paramount to be aware of data frequency shared amongst devices. We need to consider not only the amount of data produced and processed but also accessed and shared frequently by multiple entities of the IoT ecosystem.

We must be mindful that the monitoring of these devices also creates a tremendous amount of data. If we always add the alerts and other system management functions to keep these devices well-performing and available, we need to have a comprehensive performance model, including the system and service management of the complex IoT ecosystem. IoT solutions for modernisations span across data, security, application and integration architectures.

IoT Cloud for Digital Transformation

We covered the importance of Cloud Computing and the industry trends in previous chapters. As Cloud marked a paradigm shift to Information Technology and Computing field, the IoT Cloud is a critical player in the ecosystem to enable enterprise modernisation and digital transformation capabilities. The central role the Cloud plays in IoT is to facilitate the data integration of the solution components for modernisation goals.

IoT solutions are mainly used to provide real-time information to consumers. The data required to generate real-time data can be massive in scale. The Cloud, along with computing power, storage, analytics, metering, and billing components, can make this information available for our customers effectively.

One of the business value propositions of IoT for enterprise modernisation and digital transformation initiatives is the integration of Cloud to IoT, which can create new revenue streams for the organisation.

Integrating the Cloud with the IoT can create new business models enriched by real-time analysis and directly-consumed information at the same time. In other words, without the Cloud, the IoT can hardly add any value due to its real-time data and information-rich nature.

The addition of the Cloud to the IoT can also contribute to improved security, availability and performance of the IoT solutions in the modernising and transforming enterprise. Cloud providers have rigorous security, availability and performance metrics established based on a service consumption model. In particular, IoT-enabled Cloud systems seem to pose additional security measures.

Another architectural consideration is the use of Edge computing. When integrated with Edge computing, Cloud computing can add better value to the IoT ecosystem. The main reason for this is that Edge computing can do the filtering for the Cloud to focus on the usable data.

As transformation architects, we need to understand Cloud Computing architecture and how to integrate it into IoT solutions at the program level. Being aware of the transforming capabilities of Cloud technologies can be beneficial in creating large-scale commercial IoT solutions for enterprise modernisation and digital transformation initiatives.

Implications of IoT Analytics Computation

IoT solutions need computers to perform analytics and intelligence activities. Such tasks are hosted by Cloud platforms, such as analytics applications in which computation performance is essential.

We also need to consider the implication of massive data for storage platform performance. For analytics storage, we need to make an architectural decision as to whether local storage or cloud-based storage can suit our requirements. This architectural decision is necessary to address cost and performance concerns at the program level.

We can consider using IoT Analytics as a consumption-based service for cost-effectiveness. For example, AWS IoT Analytics is a fully-managed IoT analytics service that collects, pre-processes, enriches, stores and analyses IoT device data. AWS customers can also bring their custom analysis packaged in a container to execute AWS IoT Analytics. This Public Cloud offering can be beneficial to deal with the cost of the solutions for our modernisation and digital transformation goals.

As transformation architects, we also need to focus on the representation of data available to our consumers in visually compelling formats. For example, our consumers can use analytics to make sense of data, such as key performance indicators in the visualisation application in dashboards. These dashboards can include risk management views, errors, bottlenecks and view the Internet of Things in real-time.

Considering Data Lakes for IoT Data

We covered the data lakes in previous chapters hence we don't go into the details in this section. However, it is essential to highlight that IoT introduces new ways to collect data from various real-time data sources coming from the sensors of connected devices such as smart products, vehicles, and many other devices across the enterprise. This massive data creates a challenge for data management practice and platforms.

To address this challenge, using a data lake for IoT generated rich data makes it easier to store and perform analytics for IoT data.

The speed of using clean data (aggregated in a single place) for analytics can help discover ways to reduce operational costs and increase the quality of data. To this end, we need to aggregate IoT data sets in a single centralised place like data lakes.

IoT Architectural Challenges for Enterprise

There are several challenges related to IoT solutions in the enterprise modernisation and digital transformation initiatives. The challenges are multiple angles, such as architectural, technical, and non-technical. The most common architectural challenges for IoT are mobility, scalability, capacity, extendibility, interoperability, network bottlenecks, and connectivity.

Mobility is a common IoT Architecture Non-Functional aspect affecting the solutions across the enterprise and transformation programs. IoT devices need to move a lot and change their IP address and networks frequently based on their locations. For example, the routing protocols, such as RPL, must reconstruct the DODAG (Destination Oriented,

Directed Acyclic Graph) each time a node goes off the network or joins the network, which adds substantial overhead. These granular technical details, which concern mobility, may have a severe impact on solution performance, availability, security, and cost in our transformation programs.

IoT Solutions require overall scalability and capacity plans. IoT applications integrate with and serve multiple devices in the ecosystem. Managing the distribution of devices across networks and the enterprise application landscape can be complicated.

We may need a dynamic increase or decrease in capacity, coupled with vertical and horizontal scalability and extendibility of the solutions in the enterprise. IoT applications need to be tolerant of new services and devices joining the network at a fast speed. Addressing this challenge requires dynamic scalability and enormous extendibility.

Interoperability means that heterogeneous devices, solution components, elements, and protocols need to be able to work with each other harmoniously. Maintaining the interoperability in an IoT ecosystem is another challenge owing to the wealth of platforms, solution components, devices and protocols used in IoT ecosystems.

Network bottlenecks adversely affect availability, performance and the cost of products or services in productions, making the service level agreements challenging to meet. Apart from latency related to the distance, several other factors are causing the network bottlenecks. Some common causes of network bottlenecks are malfunctioning devices, having an excessive number of devices connected to the networks, limited bandwidth, and overcapacity for server utilisation.

Several other considerations also need to be made when it comes to internet connectivity related to IoT solutions in our digital transformation programs; for example, the type of Internet services, internet service providers, usage cost, and communication speed.

IoT Security and Privacy Concerns

The major IoT concerns revolve around security and privacy for the enterprise. IoT technologies are rapidly-changing, expanding and transforming to different functions and shapes; hence, IoT technologies can have a tremendous impact on security.

The previous security solutions may not meet newer solutions for the enterprise. We need fresh security approaches to address new risks, issues, and dependencies. A recent addition to IoT security is the integration of blockchain to create secure and reliable connections.

Blockchain enables the smart IoT devices to control, monitor and automate using the secure and reliable approach. Consideration of Blockchain for the enterprise modernisation and digital transformation initiatives may be beneficial to address security and privacy concerns as we mentioned in the security section in technology chapter.

Privacy is related to security. It is well-known that security risks can cause privacy issues. IoT privacy concerns are complex and complicated due to their nature; that is, they vary from country to country and are not always overt or obvious.

Therefore, to begin with, as transformation architect, we need to pay special attention to privacy requirements at the program level. Then, applying architectural rigours, such as adding privacy concerns to the architectural assessment and applying stringent risk management and mitigation process, can be very useful to address privacy concerns in our digital transformation goals.

Chapter Summary and Key Points

The main benefit and value proposition of IoT comes from collecting an enormous amount of data from various means and devices in the enterprise and then building services based on analyses of these massive amounts of data.

For digital transformation purposes, as an extended electronic ecosystem, IoT solutions can help to eliminate cumbersome technology affecting the performance of our organisations.

Considering the scalability requirements for digital transformations, we must carefully consider the amount of data produced by IoT devices.

We need to identify the number of sensors to be used and the speed of signals for these sensors in our data acquisition plan.

The IoT performance model mandates more data storage capacity, faster processes, more memory, and faster network infrastructure.

Integrating the Cloud with the IoT can create new business models enriched by real-time analysis and directly-consumed information at the same time.

Another architectural consideration is the use of Edge computing. When integrated with Edge computing, Cloud computing can add better value to the IoT ecosystem.

The speed of using clean data (aggregated in a single place) for analytics can help discover ways to reduce operational costs and increase the quality of data.

Mobility is a common IoT Architecture Non-Functional aspect affecting the solutions across the enterprise and transformation programs.

We may need a dynamic increase or decrease in capacity, coupled with vertical and horizontal scalability and extendibility of the solutions in the enterprise.

Network bottlenecks adversely affect availability, performance and the cost of products or services in productions, making the service level agreements challenging to meet.

Blockchain enables the smart IoT devices to control, monitor and automate using the secure and reliable approach.

Privacy is related to security. It is well-known that security risks can cause privacy issues. IoT privacy concerns are complex and complicated due to their nature; that is, they vary from country to country and are not always overt or obvious.

Chapter 12: Create Digital Teams

Purpose

A digital ecosystem can be consisting of many interrelated teams with a wide variety of professionals covering various facets of enterprise modernisation and digital transformation programs. We can come across many roles and responsibilities in these programs.

These roles and responsibilities need to be known and understood clearly. Stakeholder management is one of the primary responsibilities of transformation architects in digital transformation programs.

Understanding team structures, dynamics and many roles and responsibilities require a considerable amount of effort and organisation. Let's discuss these significant factors in subsequent sections starting with the talent as a crucial enabler of digital transformations.

Digital Talent

Talent is essential in enterprise modernisation and digital transformation initiatives. Therefore, as transformation architects, we need to understand the value and importance of talent for our programs. Without calibre talent, our digital programs cannot progress and transform productively.

To this end, we need to be very cautious to nurture and keep talent in our teams. We need to make every effort to retain valuable talent in our teams. We cannot emphasise enough that talent is a crucial enabler of core products and services of modernising and transforming enterprises. Without talent, an organisation cannot be competitive in its modernisation and transformation goals. There is a constant talent hunting in the industry to secure these scarce resources.

As transformation architects in our programs, we need to perform talent management and facilitation roles. We can encourage the architecting team members especially less junior team members to perform better and turn them into talented team players.

We can also pick up poor performance in our programs and help remove poorly performing employees and replace them with talented team members who can genuinely contribute to the modernisation and transformation vision. Our success depends on high-performance teams consisting of talented members.

Team Performance

Enterprise modernisation and digital transformation initiatives require team members who can perform and produce at the highest possible level. These team members must perform optimally at all times to meet the challenges of these programs. Their skills and capabilities must be tested and validated to suit the type of work they are performing in our programs.

Building high-performance teams are critical for the success of our programs. We need to create proactive and engaged local technical teams and community of practices as give back activities. These high-quality teams and collaborative community of practices can generate innovative, high-quality solutions in an accelerated manner. They are ideal contributors to modernisation and digital transformation goals.

As our teams are involved in complex transformation matters, people may have blind spots to understand the sophisticated dynamics. Blind spots can be hazardous in digital endeavours. The owner of the blind spot cannot see his or her blind spot unless using specific tools or assistance from someone else who is more experienced.

Habits and habitual thinking patterns are common causes of blind spots. Focusing on details without seeing the big picture can also cause cloudy thinking and ultimately dangerous blind spots.

However, as astute digital technical leaders, we need to look for big pictures from multiple angles and deep dive when needed hence can quickly identify blind spots and weaknesses experienced by our team members in our transformation programs.

We need to articulate situations with constructive feedback, lots of clarifying examples, metaphors, and similes. This influential articulation focus can help people to see their blind spots, understand their weaknesses, and turn them into strengths. Related to blind spots, identifying hidden agendas and hidden costs are critical for enterprise modernisation and digital transformation initiatives.

Taking necessary performance measures are essential in our transformation programs. We need to focus on both qualitative and quantitative measures for team success. We can manage across complex matrix structures in our organisations to integrate skills to our programs.

As metric oriented transformation architects, we need to use KPIs (Key Performance Indicators). We can use a team dashboard to see the trends and qualify and quantify progress in visual formats for the team members and the business stakeholders.

We need to encourage other team members to create their dashboard and shared dashboard for the team in our transformation programs. Our teams must turn our program to a data-driven organisation to measure the progress of modernisation and transformation goals structurally and methodically.

One of the key measures is customer orientation and support mechanisms. We ensure a customer-centric outlook is provided, focusing on continually improving client experience with measurable results. We are expected to be the 'thought leaders' in our transformation programs. Thought leadership is a critical need and demand in modernisation and transformation environments, for changing cultures, and transforming ecosystems.

Tangible outcomes are essential for the success of enterprise modernisation and digital transformation programs. These programs require tangible outcomes iteratively rather than monolithic. For example, some tangible outcomes can be a virtualisation of platforms, creating containers, creating reusable shared resources, reviewed products, and agreed services.

As transformation architects, we need to pay special attention to providing measurable outcomes with the support of our team members. Modernising and transforming environments present constant and rapid changes. We know that any change matters in the transforming ecosystem.

These small and rapid changes lead to more significant measurable outcomes at later stages of the modernisation and transformation; for example, the systems may need to be fully automated, loosely coupled, service-oriented, software-defined, self-learning, self-managing, and self-healing are a few to mention in this context. Now that we emphasised the importance and approach for team performance, let's get to know our key players from architectural point of view in our programs.

Technical Professionals for Transformation

As digital transformation architects, we work with many technical professionals involved in digital initiatives in our programs. For example, we closely work with architects, designers, and technical specialists. At the highest level, we work with the Enterprise Architects applying a rigorous enterprise architecture approach to help us with modernisation and digital transformation initiatives.

Let's beware that if the enterprise architecture process goes wrong in an initiative, everything else goes wrong in our transformation programs.

All other architecture types, such as solution architecture, system architecture, integration architecture, and other architecture domains, are all dependent on the quality of enterprise architecture. Apart from architecture, the subsequent activities in the modernisation and transformation lifecycle are also adversely affected.

After a validated, business-focused, and pragmatic architecture supporting the modernisation and digital transformation strategy, the design (both high level and detailed level) is the next vital aspect to be considered in the lifecycle.

As transformation architects, we participate in various forums such as the Architecture Review Boards and Design Authority forums. These forums are consisting of many architects, designers and technical specialists. For example, a Design Authority maybe consist of multiple architects with diverse expertise in different domains. Usually, Enterprise Architects orchestrate the activities with their broad knowledge and understanding of the strategy, architecture, technical matters, and business. They govern the Design Authority by using their organisational skills coupled with other architectural skills and business understanding. Let's understand the role of Enterprise Architects as we must work with them day to day basis in our transformation programs.

Enterprise Architects

Enterprise Architects have strategic, architectural thinking, and design thinking skills. These esteemed architects need to articulate the current enterprise environment to the sponsoring senior executives, set future enterprise environment goals, and show how to bridge the gap for modernisation goals between these two environments.

At a high level, Enterprise Architects understand the overall digital modernisation and transformation scope, requirements, and use cases of the solutions. Besides, Enterprise Architects perform Viability Assessments which are critical to enterprise modernisation and transformation programs. These architects must regularly assess risks, issues, dependencies and constraints considering strengths, weaknesses, opportunities and threats in their day to day tasks.

Enterprise Architects are responsible and accountable for architectural and technical governance. Technical governance is an essential aspect of modernisation initiatives. The modernisation programs require particular governance model due to their nature. A dynamic and flexible governance model is essential for modernisation initiatives. The traditional stringent and extreme rule-based oppressive governance models can be roadblocks to the progress. Agility principles best suit to the dynamic governance models.

Enterprise Architects usually perform the role of technical governance head in sizeable modernisation programs. They can have formal governance roles. For example, these architects can run the architecture review boards or design authority forums established for complex modernisation programs.

Business Domain Architects

Business Domain Architects usually assigned to a specific business domain in an enterprise and play various roles and responsibilities in digital modernisation and transformation programs.

Domain Architects can architect a component or integrated component in their business units. Even though they are business focussed, they can also have a strong technical background covering various aspects of architecture such as infrastructure, applications, data, security and more.

When we are working for a specific business unit problem, these domain architects can be instrumental in providing required guidance to our initiatives.

Infrastructure Architects

Infrastructure Architects are responsible for the underlying infrastructure such as network, servers, storage, platforms, physical facilities such as data centres and communications.

These architects are responsible for the plumbing of the digital world. As transformation architects, we closely work with the Infrastructure Architects as they are astute about the infrastructure components of our digital initiatives.

Application Architects

Application Architects are responsible for applications and middleware across the enterprise. Enterprises can have many standalone and integrated applications spanning across multiple servers, domains and geographic locations.

Application Architects understand the functionality, operability, supportability, integration, and migration of applications.

As transformation architects, we closely work with Application Architects. They are critical resources for modernisation and digital transformation programs.

Specialist Architects

This may sound like a misnomer but there are undoubtedly specialist level architects. Even though architects cover breadth, some architects specialise in particular areas in the enterprise due to the extensive scope of the domains.

The most common specialty areas for architects are Security Architect, Data Architect, Information Architect, Network Architect, Mobility Architect, Workplace Architect.

Some of these types of architects can also serve as a subject matter experts or technical specialists which we cover in the next section.

Technical Specialists

As transformation architects, we work closely with technical specialists who have distinct technology expertise covering a broad spectrum of technologies in all technical domains. These specialists are technically eminent professionals in their chosen field. In some organisations, they are called distinguished specialists.

Technical eminence or distinguished refers to outstanding technical expertise recognised internally and externally to the organisation of a technical leader who is influential and high impact to both technical and business communities.

Some technical specialists have strong industry skills, demonstrate thought leadership, and possess multiple domain expertise. These specialists are highly regarded and sought after for their views and contributions to modernisation and digital transformation initiatives.

Leading our modernisation and digital transformation programs requires distinguishing technical factors in multiple technology domains with in-depth understanding to some extent. These groups of people are ideal talents for our digital transformation programs.

Business Analysts

Even though they are not technical we closely work with the Business Analysts in architecting. Business Analysts are critical resources to translate business requirements to technical requirements working with business stakeholders, domain architects, and technical specialists.

Exceptional communication skills are essential for Business Analysts dealing with modernisation and transformation initiatives. Their communication skills are well respected and sought after by their peers, managers, and customers.

Business Analysts are expected to communicate at all levels with confidence and ease. They must articulate the most complex situations and technical matters to all stakeholders in a language that those people can understand. Business Analysts must customise their messages based on audience profile.

Digital Mentors and Coaches

Mentoring and coaching is a cultural shift and the essential requirement of modernising and transforming environments. There must be a constant nurturing and knowledge transfer from top to bottom.

To this end, as transformation architects, we must be mentors for our team members, other team members, people from partnering organisations, students from universities, and even external people in other organisations.

We need to generously share our knowledge and transfer them to anyone who needs such knowledge to utilise in modernisations and digital transformation engagements.

We also need to be good at coaching our peers, subordinates, and cross-team members by being a soundboard to them. Junior team members can be easily overwhelmed by the rapid pace changes and challenges of transformation programs.

We can be excellent listeners and even contribute to the wellbeing of our team members providing coaching sessions for stressful colleagues resulting in therapeutic outcomes. Digital transformation teams experience an enormous amount of stress especially with accelerated delivery for growing stakeholder and consumer demands.

Agile and Change Champions

Change is inevitable for enterprise modernisation and digital transformation. Everything changes continuously and rapidly. Change leadership is a vital function for modernisation and transformation. Dealing with rapid change is non-trivial, and indeed require delicate skills, experience, and insights.

As transformation architects, we must be catalysts for ongoing change and serve as an Agile Champion. With our catalytical contributions, we need to refresh the culture to more agile, collaborative, inventive, and innovative landscapes in our programs.

As change and agile champion, we can create innovative sets of practices in the transforming ecosystem. Our attributes, such as being responsive, sharing and learning mutually, and having fun with joy in a pleasant team environment, can have a tremendous impact on improving the culture for positive change in our transformation programs.

Team Learning

Learning is a never-ending process in transformational environments leading towards modernisation of legacy enterprise and digitally transforming programs. Due to changing technology stacks, process, and tools, as transformation architects, we need to learn rapidly and efficiently.

We can have a wide variety of learning styles. Based on situations and conditions, we need to learn formally and informally based on circumstances. We need to turn every possible interaction to a potential learning opportunity in our programs.

We must create learning opportunities only for ourselves but also for team members in the program. We also need to teach other people actively and on-demand. By teaching our team members, we can even learn more and better. This new way of learning is critical to meet the demands of enterprise modernisation and transformation goals.

Chapter Summary and Take Away Points

We need to be very cautious to nurture and keep talent in our teams. We need to make every effort to retain valuable talent in our teams. We cannot emphasise enough that talent is a crucial enabler of core products and services of modernising and transforming enterprises.

Building high-performance teams are critical for the success of our programs.

Habits and habitual thinking patterns are common causes of blind spots. Focusing on details without seeing the big picture can also cause cloudy thinking and ultimately dangerous blind spots.

Tangible outcomes are essential for the success of enterprise modernisation and digital transformation programs. These programs require tangible outcomes iteratively rather than monolithic.

All other architecture types, such as solution architecture, system architecture, integration architecture, and other architecture domains, are all dependent on the quality of enterprise architecture.

Enterprise Architects have strategic, architectural thinking, and design thinking skills.

Business Domain Architects usually assigned to a specific business domain in an enterprise and play various roles and responsibilities in digital modernisation and transformation programs.

Infrastructure Architects are responsible for the underlying infrastructure such as network, servers, storage, platforms, physical facilities such as data centres and communications.

Application Architects understand the functionality, operability, supportability, integration, and migration of applications.

The most common specialty areas for architects are Security Architect, Data Architect, Information Architect, Network Architect, Mobility Architect, Workplace Architect.

Specialists are technically eminent professionals in their chosen field. In some organisations, they are called distinguished specialists.

Exceptional communication skills are essential for Business Analysts dealing with modernisation and transformation initiatives.

Mentoring and coaching is a cultural shift and the essential requirement of modernising and transforming environments. There must be a constant nurturing and knowledge transfer from top to bottom.

As change and agile champion, we can create innovative sets of practices in the transforming ecosystem.

We can have a wide variety of learning styles. Based on situations and conditions, we need to learn formally and informally based on circumstances. We need to turn every possible interaction to a potential learning opportunity in our programs.

Chapter 13: Reuse and Repeat

Purpose

The purpose of this chapter is to highlight the importance of reuse and repeat the previously covered steps in this book.

Importance of Repeat

Digital transformation lifecycle is recursive with successive steps and results. There is no end to transformation. We may complete a cycle but as soon as its completion we need to deal with another cycle.

As time passes, systems get older, technology stacks become obsolete, processes get convoluted and unusable; just like human beings, everything ages in the IT systems. Therefore, we always need to modernise and transform our systems, processes, tools and technology stacks.

Due to this natural phenomenon, we added the repeat step to our digital transformation method. However, from an architectural and architecting perspective, the repeat process needs to be well structured based on a dynamic lifecycle management process.

Importance of Asset Reuse

As transformation architects, we can re-use our architectural and design assets multiple times as needed. The main reason for this is to save time and reduce the cost of rework. In addition, using established and validated building blocks of our architectural solutions can be very powerful to maintain and increase the quality requirements.

The most commonly used architectural assets are the reference architectures. We discuss reference architecture in the next section.

Reference Architectures

A reference architecture is a re-usable solution or a design in a template format. The use of a reference architecture for modernisation solutions can save us a considerable amount of time. Reference architectures are developed by experienced solution architects based on successful outcomes obtained from delivered solutions.

This means that we can trust the reference architectures as they were once successfully delivered. Following the same path as our customised specifications, these re-usable templates can save us a considerable amount of time and can improve the quality of our solutions.

As reference architectures are developed by experienced architects, they can also guide us in dealing with the unknown aspects of the solutions. Reference architectures can be used for various domains, can be combined to extend functionality and can be integrated for the final architecture solutions.

Reference architectures are developed based on the collaborative spirit in many organisations. Some architects share their experiences internally or externally for various reasons. For example, some architects share them for charitable give-back purposes or networking, or to boost their reputation and recognition in their industry. Whatever the reasons they share them, the reference architectures are invaluable resources for our planned solution architectures.

Open-source organisations produce many reference architectures in their domains. There are two primary sources for these reference architectures: either their members develop them as part of an open-source team, or some commercial companies donate their re-usable assets to the open-source organisations as reference architectures. The Open Group (TOG) is a typical example of this kind of open-source organisation.

Reference Architectures can be at a high-level or other detailed level. A typical IoT reference Architecture at a high level can include essential points, such as Portal, Dashboard, API Management, Analytics, Services, Communications, Devices, Device Management, Security Management, Infrastructure and so on. Reference Architectures are usually represented in diagrams with minimal text to explain the representations in the diagrams. Clarity is the main factor for a reference architecture. Reference Architectures usually are easy to understand and use.

As transformation architects, we need to encourage our domain and solution architects to leverage available references architectures related to enterprise modernisation and digital transformation initiatives. We also need to encourage them to create their reference architectures and share with other domain architects in our programs or the enterprise. From my experience, smart reuse of architectural assets can help reduce enterprise cost substantially.

Chapter Summary and Take Away Points

There is no end to transformation. We may complete a cycle but as soon as its completion we need to deal with another cycle.

The most commonly used architectural assets are the reference architectures.

A reference architecture is a re-usable solution or a design in a template format. The use of a reference architecture for modernisation solutions can save us a considerable amount of time.

Reference architectures are developed based on the collaborative spirit in many organisations. Some architects share their experiences internally or externally for various reasons.

Reference Architectures can be at a high-level or other detailed level. A typical IoT reference Architecture at a high level can include essential points, such as Portal, Dashboard, API Management,

Analytics, Services, Communications, Devices, Device Management, Security Management, Infrastructure and so on.

Smart reuse of architectural assets can help reduce enterprise cost substantially.

Chapter 14: Conclusions

Congratulations, we reached the conclusions after covering many facets and all steps of our digital transformation method. Now, let's take a high-level review of what we learned to reinforce our learning and comprehension. It can be useful to have a quick recap of the key points we discussed in earlier chapters with conclusive remarks.

Our digital transformation method includes 12 steps as listed below. We covered each step in a distinct chapter.

1. Establish Fundamentals

2. Simplify Complexity

3. Manage Cost

4. Innovate and Invent

5. Accelerate Delivery

6. Grow with Collaboration

7. Leverage Emerging Technology & Tools

8. Reconstruct & Modernise Data

9. Mobilise Building Blocks

10. Create Smart Objects

11. Create Digital Teams

12. Reuse and Repeat

Architectural thinking approach establishes the fundamentals and can be used as a robust framework to gain digital awareness, unfold the mystery of digital transformation, and increase our capabilities by providing a structured approach to transformation.

The structured approach is important because our brains function using structure and patterns. Understanding and accepting our current situation is crucial.

Despite all, we need to start from somewhere to identify our current environment and collect as much information as possible taking all measures.

Vision sets the scene and shows us where we want to be in the future. Our strategic vision needs to be realistic and convincing. We need to share it with all stakeholders and obtain their acceptance and approval.

Our digital strategy helps us reach our destination using a master plan. The master plan can be a high-level roadmap to take us to the destination we set. We need to proceed with a clear strategic roadmap otherwise we can get lost in the details and the constant noise.

Both users and systems have their unique and common requirements. The system requirements can be categorised under technical, support, and operational requirements. In architectural terms, requirements can be classified under two main categories, namely, functional and non-functional.

The functional requirements of a solution involve what the system offers to the consumers as functionality to be accomplished.

Non-functional aspects involve how the solutions can accomplish these functionalities, such as their performance, availability, security, reliability, scalability, usability, configuration, scalability and many more.

We use the acronym SMART to characterise requirements. SMART stands for specific, measurable, actionable, realistic and traceable.

A use case is a specific situation depicting the use of a product or service of a solution by the consumers. We develop use cases from the users' perspective. Use cases can also be determined based on roles and personas in a solution. Personas represent fictitious characters based on our knowledge of the users in the solution.

By understanding the current state and its requirements to transform, we set future state and develop a roadmap to reach the target transformation goals. The future state requires a substantial amount of analysis and predictions.

The feasibility is practised using a viability assessment work-product which is a template covering all aspects of our solution from operability perspective.

Missing this critical step in our digital solution method can result in dire consequences in the long run.

We make trade-offs to create a balance between two required yet incompatible items. In other words, a trade-off is a compromise between two options.

Re-examining our priorities, especially set by the key stakeholders for the solution objectives, can provide us useful clues and necessary guidance.

It is not possible to develop an architectural solution without taking risks. It is also possible that these risks can be turned into opportunities hence we need to mitigate them methodically and measurably.

We need to make architectural decisions very carefully and measurably. Each decision can have a severe impact and multiple implications on the solution outcomes. It may be costly to change the architectural decisions at later phases of the solution lifecycle.

Creating a solution context requires abstracting skills. We need to represent a large volume of information in small pictures by setting concise relationships amongst the components.

Some of the vital Architectural models which we can apply to the potential modernisation solutions are Component Model, Operational Model, Performance Model, Security Model, Availability Model, Services Model and Cost Model.

Use of fundamental high-level designs to see the big picture for each solution building block can be instrumental to digital transformation solutions.

System specifications need to be accurate, reliable and fast when collecting data, communicating information, sharing data and making accurate decisions.

Finding inaccurate detailed designs or wrong specifications during the implementation and production support phase can be very cost-prohibitive due to massive re-work requirements. These unexpected errors shatter the whole solution from every angle and as digital transformation architects we are the first ones who kept responsible for the consequences.

The traditional stringent and extreme rule-based or oppressive governance models can be roadblocks to the progress. One of the common frameworks for technical governance in the industry is COBIT (Control Objectives for Information and related Technology).

We know that enterprise environments can be extremely complex with multiple layers of systems, subsystems, technology stacks, tools, and processes coupled with numerous stakeholders with different agendas and consumers with different expectations.

The most common technique is simplifying complexity by using a partitioning approach. Another way of simplifying a system is reducing the number of repetitive constituents. The next technique could be moving an item from a large group of the clustered items but still, keep the relationship to preserve its core identity.

Moving with iterative steps, we can achieve some small results. Simplicity touches almost every angle of transformation solutions, as these solutions can incredibly be complex.

The positive side of this negative result is that we fail cheap, and we fail quickly. Failing cheap and quickly don't make a big difference from a financial, commercial or project schedule perspectives.

Paradoxically, to create simplicity, one needs to deal with a lot of complexity, complications and sophisticated matters.

Creating simplicity for communication requires in-depth knowledge, flexible thinking, and demonstrated skills in articulation. We must establish relationships that depict simplicity and efficiency with our stakeholders in our actions.

One of the effective ways to simplification for user-centricity is automating routine tasks and repetitive technology stacks. Automation can help standardise and simplify convoluted and repetitive tasks prone to human errors.

We need to have a specific mission to simplify the business and technology processes and make them user-centric. Simplicity and clarity are closely related. An effective way of simplifying our processes and providing simplicity to the consumer is to think like the consumers.

Applying design thinking, combined with adopting agile methods for design, is one of the simplification approaches.

The digital trends, mobile culture and agile approaches made substantial changes in addressing the cumbersome specifications, especially concerning the users or consumers.

User stories are simple templates, including the functionalities, capabilities, and specifications from users or consumers point of view.

Refraining from convoluted phrases and instead, use of precise language and explicit statements are essential factors in simplifying communication.

When authoring a document, we must be sharp and to the point with clear statements.

Because of known implications, it is critical to simplify governance framework, process and procedures for these initiatives.

One way of simplifying data is to clean it, remove duplications and errors. Reducing data sources and volumes, when needed, are also used to simplify and streamline data management processes.

Endless discussions may cloud the essential message; therefore, it is critical to control the presentation process and focus sharply on the essential points in our presentations.

We can provide simplified, clear and concise presentations without compromising the quality of content and effectiveness of the message.

Even if we create a paragon of architecture with flawless designs, if the solution is economically not viable and it does not produce a compelling return on investment, it cannot be considered as successful.

Everything in enterprise transformation generates substantial cost. There are known and hidden costs. Hidden costs are the more significant part of the proverbial iceberg.

Even though financial teams manage the cost, the technical team need to find ways to make digital solutions inexpensive, affordable and lowering the cost gradually without compromising quality.

Beware that there may be tremendous pressure from project managers and procurement staff to generate an upfront Bill of Materials due to demands of the project delivery lifecycle.

Automated SLAs can detect low availability and poor performance. These automated SLAs trigger the rules and force the organisations breaching the agreements pay the contractually agreed penalties.

We need to pay attention to the SLAs from the nascent stages of the digital solution lifecycle. The higher the quality of the solutions, the easier it is for SLAs to meet when the solutions are in production and the operational state.

Enterprise digital systems can include business IT processes, business data, business applications, IT infrastructure, and IT service delivery. These domains can even be more complicated with the addition of geographical factors such as adding multiple countries to the equation.

We can define innovative and inventive thinking as the use of creativity for generating novel ideas, new methods, new approaches, new techniques, new processes, and new tools or improve the current environment to gain insights, add compelling business value, reduce unnecessary costs, and increase desired revenue by focussing on return on investment from our digital transformation endeavours.

Innovation and invention require multiple modes of thinking differently. Binary thinking consists of simple terms such as yes or no, black and white, good or bad. This type of thinking can be useful in a certain context however it has its limitations for qualitative assessment requirements.

Some commonly used techniques for horizontal thinking are randomisations, distortions, reversals, exaggerations, metaphors, analogies, dreaming, theme mining, questioning the norms, and creating contradictions. Using these techniques opens new opportunities for our creativity.

In transforming organisations, innovation and invention become habitual. Our team members strive for excellence by creating new ideas in their day to day tasks. No one is called weird names or with other judgemental adjectives.

Design thinking allows the team to be intuitive and logical at the same time. Design thinking enables team members to be more creative to recognise new patterns. We apply design thinking to our digital transformation activities at all times.

We must also have customer-centric mindset and put ourselves in customers' shoes with strong empathy.

Many innovations and inventions can be co-created with clients. Co-creation can be seen as a win-win situation for both the service providers and their consumers.

One way of dealing with resisting people is to be transparent to them and have a close face to face conversations. We must find ways to engage those types of team members and show the value and benefit of new ideas which can benefit them.

One of the workaround solutions can be to separate new and old business as usual as two different departments. However, we must find some collaborative ways to bridge them.

We also need to watch out cumbersome business processes which can be deterrent factors for innovation and invention goals for transforming environments.

As transformation architects, we need to embrace agile delivery and make it as part of our transforming culture.

Whist dealing with legacy IT footprint to understand it in an agile manner, we also need to have the vision of well-functioning solutions and put our energies on rapid-paced iterative modernisation and digital transformation initiatives.

Speed to market is one of the most fundamental requirements of digital transformation initiatives. We can generate revenues only by acting very quickly in this competitive world.

There appears to be some comfort zone created for using waterfall methods in traditional organisations.

Accelerated delivery for digital transformations requires multiple roles and responsibilities. The most common roles in agile teams are the scrum master, the product owner, and the scrum team member.

Providing an effective acceptance criterion can lead the team to think in the right direction.

To address the fear of architecture and designs, we can apply pragmatic architecture in fast-paced modernisations and digital transformation initiatives in our programs.

Pragmatism negates perfectionism. The notion of perfection equates to failure in fast-paced digital transformation programs.

Taking extended times is not feasible in this digital age any more.

We can see the architecture development like product development. Use of evolving methods such as DevOps is also prime considerations for accelerating delivery of software development products for substantial digital transformation initiatives.

Applying automation and standardisation to our digital transformation objectives, we can reduce the number of resources required to maintain manual and tedious tasks.

Accelerated delivery for digital transformations requires removing silos in enterprises. A siloed culture can also impact the quality of the products due to a lack of integrated views.

Another undesirable implication of having silos is that some departments in these traditional settings in the same organisations even compete with each other.

We cannot emphasise enough that as transformation architects, we must focus on the priority items in the digital transformation backlogs based on precise priority orders set by our transformation strategy and aligned with our delivery goals and objectives.

A sprint is the shortest time bombed duration to create the minimum viable product. A sprint duration usually a two to three-week period. This limited-time speeds up delivery and encourages the team to focus on the priority items to create the minimum viable product.

Accelerated delivery empowered by an agile approach mandates the principles of the fail fast, fail early, and fail cheaply.

By delivering rapidly and in agility, we make our projects profitable and contribute to generate more revenue from accelerated delivery.

Through incremental progress, prioritised backlog management, speedy iterative delivery through sprints, we can prevent the cost of failure for big chunks of work items and more importantly, we can turn the costs into revenues.

In its true meaning, collaboration refers to a team of people working together for mutual goals to achieve successful and synergetic outcomes.

Collaboration is essential to create synergy in digital transformation teams.

Fusion principles aim to bring individuals from various backgrounds, small groups with different purposes, various teams with differing capabilities, communities of practices with different missions under a single umbrella for serving a joint mission.

We don't wait for fusion to happen by itself. We know that nothing can happen by itself. Naturally, someone with leadership and architectural skills must initiate it.

Written communications can create some challenges, such as a careless piece of writing may cause some offence and kill the spirit of collaboration.

The magic of fusion starts with these repetitions. Successful repetitions make ripple effects for more success.

Diversity oriented magical aspect of fusion and collaboration leading to innovation is an ideal situation for transforming the enterprise.

Influence is particularly essential to create a collaborative culture in modernising and transforming our legacy environments.

Our vision, strategy, knowledge, skills, actions have an impact on our credibility. Our architecting goals and our organisations' business goals must align with these critical attributes.

Diverse ideas ignite and accelerate innovation. With this approach, we can create new options and choices. Connecting those choices and options also make a ripple effect on the culture.

Broad technology awareness is a mandatory attribute for digital transformation architects.

The key technology enablers of enterprise modernisation and digital transformation goals are Cloud Computing, Mobile technologies, IoT, Big Data, and AI-based or Cognitive Data Analytics.

The most significant attribute of Cloud is that the cloud service model can expand or reduce computer resources based on service requirements.

'Pay per use' or 'pay as you go' is another essential characteristic that Cloud services model offers.

Flexible workload movement is another crucial attribute of Cloud service model. There may be times an organisation requires to run their workloads in a different time zone, and the workloads can easily be moved to a data centre in another country.

Some believe that the IoT can be as important as the emergence of the internet itself. Some even point out that it can be the next big thing in our lives.

Even though architecturally similar to traditional data, Big Data requires newer methods and tools to deal with data.

The Big Data process refers to capturing a substantial amount of data from multiple sources, storing analysing, searching, transferring, sharing, updating, visualising and governing huge volumes data sets such as in petabytes or even exabytes nowadays.

The descriptive analytics deals with situations such as what is happening right now based on incoming data. The predictive analytics refers to what might happen in the future. Prescriptive analytics deals with actions to be taken. Diagnostic analytics ask the question of why something happened. Each analytics type serves difference scenarios and use-cases.

AI-based Big Data Analytics is a comprehensive business-driven discipline. At a high level, it aims to make quick business decisions, reduce the cost for a product or service, and test new market to create new products and services.

We can better understand Big data analytics looking at its inherent characteristics such as connection, conversion, cognition, configuration, content, customisation, cloud, cyber, and community. These terms are associated with our day to day architectural practices and self-explanatory hence we don't go into details here.

Machine learning refers to computer systems to learn and improve based on their learning from the analysis of large volumes of data sets without programming. It is part of the artificial intelligence domain in computer science.

Text analytics leverage machine learning, computational linguistics, and traditional statistical analysis. Text analytics focus on converting massive volumes of a machine or human-generated text into meaningful structures to create business insights and support business decision-making.

Text summarisation is another widely used unstructured data processing technique which can automatically create a condensed summary of a document or selected groups of documents.

NLP is commonly used in various commercial products such as Siri by Apple, Watson by IBM, and Alexa by Amazon products.

Cybersecurity touches every aspect of enterprise modernisation and digital transformation initiatives.

The Blockchain is based on decentralised technology framework. It is digital data management protocol with a network consists of nodes. It offers storage technology coupled with information transmission. The Blockchain protocol is based on peer-to-peer. In other words, it does not require a control body. The primary use case for Blockchain is identity management.

Networks are enablers of Cloud, IoT, Blockchain, and Big Data analytics. It is so fundamental that these technology stacks cannot perform and even cannot exist without a network.

Mobility is a critical interrelated technology domain in digitally transforming organisations moving to mobile solutions.

We also need to understand the domain of Enterprise Mobile Management. This domain includes essential components such as device management, application management, content management, email management, and unified endpoint management.

One of the best representations of IT Service model is implemented using popular ITIL (Information Technology Infrastructure Library.

Applying data intelligence steers the transformation and leads to new business insights. One significant fact is that data, especially Big Data, is ubiquitous in every enterprise.

Big data is different from traditional data. The main differences come from characteristics such as volume, velocity, variety, veracity, value and overall complexity of data sets in a data platform or overall ecosystem.

The Big Data process refers to capturing a substantial amount of data from multiple sources, storing analysing, searching, transferring, sharing, updating, visualising and governing huge volumes data in the magnitude of petabytes or even exabytes.

At a high level, the data management lifecycle can include foundations, acquisitions, preparation, input, processing, output, interpretation, analytics, consumptions, retention, backup, recovery, archival, and destruction.

This first layer includes legacy data sources, new data sources, master data hubs, reference data hubs, and content repositories. The second layer includes data ingestion, operational information, landing area, analytics zone, archive, real-time analytics, exploration, integrated warehouse, data mart zones. The third layer is the analytics platform. It consists of real-time analytics, planning, forecasting, decision making, predictive analytics, data discovery, visualisations, dashboard, and other analytics features. The fourth layer consists of outputs such as business processes, decision-making schemes, and point of interactions.

Business vocabulary provides consistent terms to be used by the whole organisation. Business departments own business vocabulary.

For the Big Data governance, we need to consider essential factors such as security, privacy, trust, operability, conformance, agility, innovation and transformation of data. Big Data governance is a broad area and covers components, scope, requirements handling, strategy, architecture, design, development, analysis, tests, processing, components, relationships, input, output, business goals, insights, and all other aspects of data management and analytics.

We can define data lakes in the simplest terms as the dynamically clean and instantly useable data sources made available for specific purposes. Data lakes are dynamic stores and can be fed iteratively as further clean data are discovered and transformed from multiple sources in the enterprise. Designing data lakes require critical consideration of data types.

Big Data solutions are distinct and require additional expertise. In addition to considering several architectural points, these solutions also require domain knowledge of data and information architecture.

Modularity is another essential consideration for Big Data solutions for digital transformation goals.

In addition to legacy data sources, we need to consider new data sources in Big Data modernisation and digital transformation solutions.

Open source is incredibly useful and widespread for information technology hence equally crucial for data analytics in the enterprise. It is a type licensing agreement which allows the developers and users to freely use the software, modify it, develop new ways to improve it and integrate to larger projects.

Some of the most popular Big Data and Analytics platforms with associated tools are Google BigQuery, Hortonworks Data Platform, HP Bigdata, IBM Big Data, Microsoft Azure, SAP Bigdata Analytics, Teradata Bigdata Analytics, Amazon Web Services.

Mobility involves people, process, technology and tools at a massive scale in every organisation. Mobility is essential for people and their work engagements in the enterprise.

Lifecycle management for mobile devices is an essential architectural consideration in enterprise modernisation and digital transformation initiatives.

One of the primary challenges related to the lifecycle of mobile devices is dealing with quantity.

Security control of the data can be daunting too. These security implications cross the data and application domains; hence, a collaborative effort among the Security, Data and Application Architects are required.

Product and service providers widely use Mobile BI. Some established and popular Mobile BI environments are publicly accessible services such as Appstore by Apple, Google Play Store, and Samsung Galaxy Store.

A unified endpoint management (UEM) practice is essential for enterprise modernisation and digital transformation initiatives. UEM includes relevant software tools and centralised management interfaces for consumers.

We cannot transform our legacy enterprise without including the mobility to the equation.

The main benefit and value proposition of IoT comes from collecting an enormous amount of data from various means and devices in the enterprise and then building services based on analyses of these massive amounts of data.

For digital transformation purposes, as an extended electronic ecosystem, IoT solutions can help to eliminate cumbersome technology affecting the performance of our organisations.

Considering the scalability requirements for digital transformations, we must carefully consider the amount of data produced by IoT devices.

We need to identify the number of sensors to be used and the speed of signals for these sensors in our data acquisition plan.

The IoT performance model mandates more data storage capacity, faster processes, more memory, and faster network infrastructure.

Integrating the Cloud with the IoT can create new business models enriched by real-time analysis and directly-consumed information at the same time.

Another architectural consideration is the use of Edge computing. When integrated with Edge computing, Cloud computing can add better value to the IoT ecosystem.

The speed of using clean data (aggregated in a single place) for analytics can help discover ways to reduce operational costs and increase the quality of data.

Mobility is a common IoT Architecture Non-Functional aspect affecting the solutions across the enterprise and transformation programs.

We may need a dynamic increase or decrease in capacity, coupled with vertical and horizontal scalability and extendibility of the solutions in the enterprise.

Network bottlenecks adversely affect availability, performance and the cost of products or services in productions, making the service level agreements challenging to meet.

Blockchain enables the smart IoT devices to control, monitor and automate using the secure and reliable approach.

Privacy is related to security. It is well-known that security risks can cause privacy issues. IoT privacy concerns are complex and complicated due to their nature; that is, they vary from country to country and are not always overt or obvious.

We need to be very cautious to nurture and keep talent in our teams. We need to make every effort to retain valuable talent in our teams. We cannot emphasise enough that talent is a crucial enabler of core products and services of modernising and transforming enterprises.

Building high-performance teams are critical for the success of our programs.

Habits and habitual thinking patterns are common causes of blind spots. Focusing on details without seeing the big picture can also cause cloudy thinking and ultimately dangerous blind spots.

Tangible outcomes are essential for the success of enterprise modernisation and digital transformation programs. These programs require tangible outcomes iteratively rather than monolithic.

All other architecture types, such as solution architecture, system architecture, integration architecture, and other architecture domains, are all dependent on the quality of enterprise architecture.

Enterprise Architects have strategic, architectural thinking, and design thinking skills. Business Domain Architects usually assigned to a specific business domain in an enterprise and play various roles and responsibilities in digital modernisation and transformation programs. Infrastructure Architects are responsible for the underlying infrastructure such as network, servers, storage, platforms, physical facilities such as data centres and communications. Application Architects understand the functionality, operability, supportability, integration, and migration of applications. The most common specialty areas for architects are Security Architect, Data Architect, Information Architect, Network Architect, Mobility Architect, Workplace Architect.

Specialists are technically eminent professionals in their chosen field. In some organisations, they are called distinguished specialists.

Exceptional communication skills are essential for Business Analysts dealing with modernisation and transformation initiatives.

Mentoring and coaching is a cultural shift and the essential requirement of modernising and transforming environments. There must be a constant nurturing and knowledge transfer from top to bottom.

As change and agile champion, we can create innovative sets of practices in the transforming ecosystem.

We can have a wide variety of learning styles. Based on situations and conditions, we need to learn formally and informally based on circumstances. We need to turn every possible interaction to a potential learning opportunity in our programs.

There is no end to transformation. We may complete a cycle but as soon as its completion we need to deal with another cycle.

The most commonly used architectural assets are the reference architectures. A reference architecture is a re-usable solution or a design in a template format. The use of a reference architecture for modernisation solutions can save us a considerable amount of time.

Reference architectures are developed based on the collaborative spirit in many organisations. Some architects share their experiences internally or externally for various reasons.

Reference Architectures can be at a high-level or other detailed level. A typical IoT reference Architecture at a high level can include essential points, such as Portal, Dashboard, API Management, Analytics, Services, Communications, Devices, Device Management, Security Management, Infrastructure and so on. Smart reuse of architectural assets can help reduce enterprise cost substantially.

I attempted to show significant aspects and valuable considerations for architecting digital transformation with proven 12-step method. I hope you found the method and the framework easy to follow and the content concise, uncluttered, informative, and easy-to-read.

You may have experienced an overemphasis on the architectural rigour in this book which is on purpose. We cannot compromise the rigour aiming to the quality of products and services as a target outcome for modernisation and digital transformation goals in the enterprise. However, there must be a delicate balance among architectural rigour, business value, and speed to market.

Applying a pragmatic approach to multiple substantial transformation initiatives and complex modernisations programs has been beneficial for me. The key point is using an incrementally progressing iterative approach to every aspect of modernisation and transformation initiatives, including people, processes, tools, and technologies as a whole.

I have full confidence that this book provided valuable insights into the broad topic of architecting digital transformations.

Appendix: Other Books in this Series

A Practical Guide for IoT Solution Architects

Architecting secure, agile, economic, highly available, well-performing IoT ecosystems

The focus of this book is to provide IoT solution architects with practical guidance and a unique perspective. Solution architects working in IoT ecosystems have an unprecedented level of responsibility at work; therefore, dealing with IoT ecosystems can be daunting.

As an experienced practitioner of this topic, I understand the challenges faced by the IoT solution architects. In this book, I have reflected upon my insights based on my solution architecture experience spread across three decades. In addition, this book can also guide other architects and designers who want to learn the architectural aspects of IoT and understand the key challenges and practical resolutions in IoT solution architectures. Each chapter focuses on the key aspects that form the framing scope for this book; namely, security, availability, performance, agility, and cost-effectiveness.

In this book, I have also provided useful definitions, a brief practical background on IoT and a guiding chapter on solution architecture development. The content is mainly practical; hence, it can be applied or be a supplemental input to the architectural projects at hand.

Architecting Big Data Solutions Integrated with IoT & Cloud

Create strategic business insights with agility

IoT, Big Data, and Cloud Computing are three distinct technology domains with overlapping use cases. Each technology has its own merits; however, the combination of three creates a synergy and the golden opportunity for businesses to reap the exponential benefits. This combination can create technological magic for innovation when adequately architected, designed, implemented, and operated.

Integrating Big Data with IoT and Cloud architectures provide substantial business benefits. It is like a perfect match. IoT collects real-time data. Big Data optimises data management solutions. Cloud collects, hosts, computes, stores, and disseminates data rapidly.

Based on these compelling business propositions, the primary purpose of this book is to provide practical guidance on creating Big Data solutions integrated with IoT and Cloud architectures. To this end, the book offers an architectural overview, solution practice, governance, and underlying technical approach for creating integrated Big Data, Cloud, and IoT solutions.

The book offers an introduction to solution architecture, three distinct chapters comprising Big Data, Cloud, and the IoT with the final chapter, including conclusive remarks to consider for Big Data solutions. These chapters include essential architectural points, solution practice, methodical rigour, techniques, technologies, and tools.

Creating Big Data solutions are complex and complicated from multiple angles. However, with the awareness and guidance provided in this book, the Big Data solutions architects can be empowered to provide useful and productive solutions with growing confidence.

A Technical Excellence Framework for Innovative Digital Transformation Leadership

Transform enterprise with technical excellence, innovation, simplicity, agility, fusion, and collaboration

The primary purpose of this book is to provide valuable insights for digital transformational leadership empowered by technical excellence by using a pragmatic five-pillar framework. This empowering framework aims to help the reader understand the common characteristics of technical and technology leaders in a structured way.

Even though there are different types of leaders in broad-spectrum engaging in digital transformations, in this book, we only concentrate on excellent technical and technology leaders having digital transformation goals to deal with technological disruptions and robust capabilities to create new revenue streams. No matter whether these leaders may hold formal executive titles or just domain specialist titles, they demonstrate vital characteristics of excellent technical leadership capabilities enabling them to lead complex and complicated digital transformation initiatives.

The primary reason we need to understand technical excellence and required capabilities for digital transformational leadership in a structured context is to model their attributes and transfer the well-known characteristics to the aspiring leaders and the next generations. We can transfer our understanding of these capabilities at an individual level and apply them to our day to day activities. We can even turn them into useful habits to excel in our professional goals. Alternatively, we can pass this information to other people that we are responsible for, such as our teenagers aiming for digital leadership roles, tertiary students, mentees, and colleagues.

We attempt to define the roles of strategic technical and technology leaders using a specific framework, based on innovation, simplicity, agility, collaboration, fusion and technical excellence. This framework offers a common understanding of the critical factors of the leader. The structured analysis presented in this book can be valuable to understand the contribution of technical leaders clearly.

Admittedly, this book has a bias towards the positive attributes of excellent leaders on purpose. The compelling reason for this bias is to focus on the positive aspects and describe these attributes concisely in an adequate amount to grasp the topic so that these positive attributes can be reused and modelled by the aspiring leaders. As the other side of the coin is also essential for different insights, I plan to deal with the detrimental aspects of useless leaders in a separate book, perhaps under the lessons learned context considering different use cases for a different audience type. Consequently, I excluded the negative aspects of useless leaders in this book.

A Modern Enterprise Architecture
Approach Empowered with Cloud, Mobility,
IoT & Big Data

Modernise enterprise with pragmatic architecture, powerful technologies, innovative agility, and fusion

I authored this book to provide essential guidance, compelling ideas, and unique ways to Enterprise Architects so that they can successfully perform complex enterprise modernisation initiatives transforming from chaos to coherence. This is not an ordinary theory book describing Enterprise Architecture in detail. There are myriad of books on the market and in libraries discussing details of enterprise architecture.

As a practising Senior Enterprise Architect, myself, I read hundreds of those books and articles to learn different views. They have been valuable to me to establish my foundations in the earlier phase of my profession. However, what is missing now is a concise guidance book showing Enterprise Architects the novel approaches, insights from the real-life experience and experimentations, and pointing out the differentiating technologies for enterprise modernisation. If only there were such a guide when I started engaging in modernisation and transformation programs. The biggest lesson learned is the business outcome of the enterprise modernisation. What genuinely matters for business is the return on investment of the enterprise architecture and its monetising capabilities. The rest is the theory because nowadays sponsoring executives, due to economic climate, have no interest, attention, or tolerance for non-profitable ventures. I am sorry for disappointing some idealistic Enterprise Architects, but with due respect, it is the reality, and we cannot change it. This book deals with reality rather than theoretical perfection. Anyone against this view on this climate must be coming from another planet. In this concise, uncluttered and easy-to-read book, I attempt to show the significant pain points and valuable considerations for enterprise modernisation using a structured approach. The architectural rigour is still essential. We cannot compromise the rigour aiming to the quality of products and services as a target outcome. However, there must be a delicate balance among architectural rigour, business value, and speed to market. I applied this pragmatic approach to multiple substantial transformation initiatives and complex modernisations programs. The key point is using an incrementally progressing iterative approach to every aspect of modernisation initiatives, including people, processes, tools, and technologies as a whole. Starting with a high-level view of enterprise architecture to set the context, I provided a dozen of distinct chapters to point out and elaborate on the factors which can make a real difference in dealing with complexity and producing excellent modernisation initiatives. As eminent leaders, Enterprise Architects are the critical talents who can undertake this massive mission using their people and technology skills, in addition to many critical attributes such as calm and composed approach. They are architects, not firefighters. I have full confidence that this book can provide valuable insights and aha moments for these talented architects to tackle this enormous mission turning chaos to coherence.

Digital Intelligence: A framework to digital transformation capabilities

I authored this book because dealing with intelligence, and the digital world is a passion for me and wanted to share my passion with you. In this book,

I aim to provide compelling ideas and unique ways to increase, enhance, and deepen your digital intelligence and awareness and apply them to your organisation's digital journey particularly for modernisation and transformation initiatives. I used the architectural thinking approach as the primary framework to convey my message.

Based on my architectural thought leadership on various digital transformation and modernisation engagements, with the accumulated wealth of knowledge and skills, I want to share these learnings in a concise book hoping to add value by contributing to the broader digital community and the progressing initiatives.

Rest assured, this is not a theory or an academic book. It is purely practical and based on lessons learned from real enterprise transformation and modernisation initiatives taken in large corporate environments. I made every effort to make this book concise, uncluttered, and easy-to-read by removing technical jargons for a broader audience who want to enhance digital intelligence and awareness.

Upfront, this book is not about a tool, application, a single product, specific technology, or service, and certainly not to endorse any of these items. However, this book focuses on architectural thinking and methodical approach to improve digital intelligence and awareness. It is not like typical digital transformation books available on the market. In this book, I do not cover and repeat the same content of those books describing digital transformations. My purpose is different.

What distinguishes this book from other books is that I provide an innovative thinking framework and a methodical approach to increase your digital quotient based on experience, aiming not to sell or endorse any products or services even though I mention some prominent technologies which enable digital transformation, for your digital awareness, intelligence, and capabilities.